Editorial

Stewart Conn turned 70 last year, his birthday celebrated in style with a party run by Shore Poets last November. We add our huzzah to the cheers with the special feature here. Having lost most of that elder generation in the Muse, we keenly embrace him in the role played by MacCaig, Iain Crichton Smith, Sorley MacLean, Hamish Henderson & co. The literary lot needs to look to likes of Stewart for support, for a wigging if we need it, to someone who naturally holds that moral and artistic authority, and has remained true to what matters all his life. We have that in Stewart.

We've had it for a long time, in fact, though Stewart is a quiet, modest man who doesn't "sidle backwards into the limelight" (mischieviously said by MacCaig of A N Other!). As the pamphlet *There's a Poem to be Made* shows, (see pg 81) many poets – Christine De Luca, Gerry Cambridge, Allan Crosbie, Ian McDonough – owe much to his inspiration – and in various capacities, he gave huge support to the elder bunch too, especially Iain Crichton Smith. Working with him has been a delight: his help, interest and refreshing child-like joy at progress has been wonderful.

Another very similar poet is Meg Bateman. She shares Stewart's modesty, his sense of responsibility to other writers, and the community, playing her part by working as an anthologist, and at Sabhal Mor Ostaig. Both are untainted by the 'swellt heid syndrome' which afflicts some writers, especially those vaunted by fashion and the media. Both have a hot line to 'the lyric muse' and write best when stimulated by sudden, unpredictable illumination. Both are vicious tigresses when faced with the unacceptable (Stewart's farewell speech to the BBC famously Bollocked the Boffins for their Thatcherite ways). Neither have had due recognition, and both would have remained unspoiled by it had they had it.

Scottish PEN, founded in 1927 by Helen B Cruickshank, Hugh MacDiarmid and others, is 80 this year. Having served on its committee, I have always marvelled at what it manages to do, funded largely by the ether. PEN campaigns for oppressed and marginalised writers, promotes freedom of expression and international co-operation. Muriel Spark (see Stewart's essay on her poetry) hallmarked it as evoking a "sense of our unquestionably being born free", its principles "especially natural to the Scottish character with its independent mindedness". Thanks to ex-president, Tessa Ransford, PEN at last got its hands on dosh from some worldly organisations – and found a good home in the Writers' Museum. The mantle now passes to Jenni Calder who has also kindly provided poems by her father, David Daiches, and photographs, for this issue.

The PEN exhibition opens 10 March in the Writers' Museum. Other events are planned – details on www.scottishpen.org. Few organisations are worthier (without the yawns) than PEN, and its Scottish branch has distinguished itself in being hyper-active in many a good cause.

Meg Bateman – A Gratuitous Exhibitionist?

Interviewed by Richard King

Meg Bateman was born in Scotland in 1959. She has two solo collections: Òrain Ghaoil *(1990) and* Aotromachd agus Dàin Eile *(1997). The latter won a Scottish Arts Council Award and was short-listed for Scottish Book of the Year. Her poems have been published in journals, collections, and anthologies. She lives on Skye, teaching at Sabhal Mòr Ostaig and is an Honorary Senior Lecturer at St Andrews University. She is a scholar, translator, reviewer, lecturer and poet in both Gaelic and English, holding a PhD in Classical Gaelic religious poetry. Meg spoke with Richard King after a reading in St Andrews on 18 November 2004.*

Richard King: *In your reading you mentioned Ted Hughes's notion that poets write on a single theme. What is your theme?*

Meg Bateman: Optimism about humanity. I made this up just now. [laughs] Frustrated love poems, which are mostly what my collection *Aotromachd* contains, were written because I was frustrated that things could be better than they were, if communication were clearer. Which means somehow that we, humanity, can be more accepting of each other. Do you have a notion of what my one theme might be?

RK: Many of your poems are about loss, yet not really about the lost love, man, deer, Gaelic, etc., but a loss in the narrator. Perhaps departure and movement is your theme, where something has left and the beauty of it is being described?

MB: Yes, maybe that's it. If I weren't optimistic that things could be better, then many situations wouldn't be so painful. A complaint is an insistence that things have the potential to be better. When I was up for the Scottish Book of the Year, one of the judges called me the "Laureate of Loss". [laughs] I think that sounds very sad. I don't feel they're that sad, actually, because the sadness points to what could be on the other side of the curtain. I'm glad when people say my poems are funny. I think my poems are quite ironic. There's one poem, 'Ròs/ Rose', about a man who's gone away. The narrator thinks how the man is now lying in another woman's arms and another woman is kissing him with triumphant lips. I wrote that ironically. I don't see a love relationship as a unique combination of two. I see it more as a moveable feast! So when someone characterises me as a 'Laureate of Loss', I'm a little bit taken aback.

When I discovered that the *Aotromachd* books were out of print, I thought I should produce another collection. So I've been working on a new volume. People have criticised me for not writing about this and that, perhaps not being socially aware. They ask, "Where are your poems about the Iraqi War, about Mr Bush and Mr Blair?" It's not that I don't think about them, have strong feelings about them, but they're not poetic feelings. I don't want to write versified dogma.

RK: Might readers in Gaelic interpret your poetic themes differently than readers in English?

MB: This is inevitable because anyone who knows Gaelic is sensitive to a different armament of images from English readers, and words will have different connotations. Man's relationship with the land is quite different in the Gaelic mind from the English reading, post-Romantic mind. But that each person is likely to interpret poems differently from someone else depending on what experience is brought to a poem.

RK: You said that you're shy with people one-on-one, but reading poems to an audience can be cathartic. Why?

MB: Poetry isn't a social discourse. When you're speaking in groups of people, or to an individual, you're very aware of the other person, of their barriers and sensibilities, of what can be crossed, what cannot. When reading poetry I speak more frankly, more honestly. You don't speak about the weather when you're writing poetry.

A couple of other poets and I participated in a conference recently on poetry and the human spirit. It was organised by Richard Holloway and the Scottish Churches' House. Holloway was an Episcopalian Archbishop, but he has become increasingly agnostic through his life, and he is agnostic now. He's retired, so he doesn't have to square being an archbishop and an agnostic. He suggests that poetry may be a more honest way of guiding the human spirit than the Judeo-Christian scripts from a pre-scientific age. I think that poetry is often secular prayer. It's bringing the best out in you. It's asking yourself the deepest questions, but it's not thirled to any one dogmatic system. I don't think many of my poems come from a spirit of meanness. I draw them out of my deepest reserves.

RK: You are a poet who writes in both English and Gaelic. You're a translator, scholar, reviewer, and lecturer in both languages. When you write a poem, how do you decide what language it will be in?

MB: I like to create in Gaelic. I'm not a native speaker. My sense of what I want in poetry, my poetic aesthetics, was formed through Gaelic examples. I was quite old, in the age of poets, when I started writing, in my early twenties. It was during that vacant unfocused time, when I was starting a PhD that poems would gel. Because the examples I looked at as an undergraduate were Gaelic and my chief inspiration, Sorley MacLean, wrote in Gaelic, it seemed natural that I would write in Gaelic, too.

When a poem is coming to me, I wouldn't say it comes in any language, but as a tension, an awareness of a paradox. And to put any words on that tension is a sort of translation, whether Gaelic or English. Poems come at inconvenient moments, like when you're in the bath, and if I write down anything at all, I could well do it in a mixture of the two languages. Then I work on it in Gaelic. There is much more work in my Gaelic poems than in the English translations. I like the medium of Gaelic. It's got long sounds and short sounds, and the normal form of rhyme is assonance. It feels very pliable. And I like the texture of it, if texture is the right metaphor. So I work away on the Gaelic and when it's right, I translate it to English. But the act of translating it into English makes me see it from a different perspective, then I go back and change the Gaelic again, back and forth, back and forth. In the end I think both versions are better than if I had had only one window to look through.

I got a questionnaire from a young woman about translation, and I got very confused. I realize the question isn't as simple as I thought. She was asking me things like, 'Do I look at it as a double creation or am I quite happy to have my Gaelic translated by somebody else?' I think I'm closer to the double creation. There are quite a lot of poets who make a political point of getting someone else to translate their poems to prove, I think, that they are independent poems. I usually prefer my own translations.

I think the waters are further muddied in that I'm a learner. And as a learner there are risks I cannot take because they would be construed as mistakes. Readers would say 'she made a mistake', when in fact I might have done it on purpose! You can't play with words if you're a learner. [laughs] Or maybe you could if you had more courage.

RK: *Gaelic poet Christopher Whyte wrote that Gaelic has never really had a modern, urban, industrial life, "it has never been adopted by a bourgeoisie". Do you agree? And does this make your translation, this double creation, difficult when some of the words perhaps don't exist in Gaelic?*

MB: Yes, I think Christopher Whyte is mostly right in that there's not a home-grown Gaelic-speaking city. But outwith the Gaelic area there are as many Gaelic speakers living in urban areas as there are living within the Highlands, and most of them are living in Glasgow. One Gaelic poet who made a lot of songs was Donald MacIntyre, nick-named Donald Paisley because that's where he was from.

My poetic voice has been conditioned through Gaelic. There's not as many abstract nouns, not so many culturally specific words. I can't write poems full of particular cultural allusions in Gaelic because it doesn't have such a big cultural hinterland to call on. So I think that Gaelic has conditioned my poetic voice to think in concrete, non-abstract terms, in simple timeless images, often natural rather than urban. Sometimes I do write a poem in English because what I've picked up on is the tastiness of people's ways of speaking in English. I wrote one just recently set in a Glasgow guitar shop where I've got Glaswegians speaking. I won't be translating that into Gaelic. There wouldn't be any point.

I think I'm a little more honest about it now than I used to be. I used to think of myself as a Gaelic poet. I would probably look out for things that were manageable in Gaelic. I'm more relaxed about it now. My next book will contain some poems that are in English only. And one or two in

Gaelic only, too. Quite a lot depends on the atmosphere of each language.

RK: *In your poem "The Decline of Gaelic" you revised a few lines and changed the title of your earlier "The Loss of Gaelic," yet the Gaelic translation stayed the same. Could you talk about this process?*

MB: 'Loss' was too final a word. Loss can mean total loss, or it can mean a reduction, can't it? But it was for fear that people might read the title as meaning a total loss that made me change it to 'Decline' which has the sense of the Gaelic 'sìoladh'. It was an early poem. I do tend to go for the concrete and the simple, rather than the abstract, and if possible, I avoid Latinate words, but I made an exception here in settling on 'decline'.

Gaelic is a dying language. It's inevitable for it to die out, unlike Welsh. In Scotland Gaelic isn't a clear marker of identity. People are as happy to use their history, the geography and their way of life as that mark. There's not enough of a groundswell of native speakers wanting Gaelic to survive to give much hope that it will do so.

RK: *Why not let it go?*

MB: There are people who say 'let it go'. There are some native speakers, for whom Gaelic represents the old way of life, with now dead parents, and they would sooner let it die gracefully, than garbled in the mouth of a learner or just started up in children's Gaelic programmes where everybody screams like they scream in English language programmes. I'm not a legislative person. I can see where they're coming from. And I have a certain degree of sympathy with that view.

The scholar Joshua Fishman says language is the primary mark of identity. We can easily think of a world where people are bilingual, with a *lingua franca* for communicating with the outside world, and another language in which we vest our values, our sense of community and identity. Fishman says that supporting minority languages isn't against modernity, but part of modernity. It is letting the individual be more important than the state, and letting human values be more important than the market and technological forces.

RK: *So why doesn't Scotland consider Gaelic as a clear marker of its identity?*

MB: There are a lot of mixed associations with Gaelic. There have been the clearances, emigration, poverty. I've heard lots of people say, "Gaelic held me back; I don't want it to hold my children back". People have associated a Highland accent with poverty, slowness. There seems an antagonism towards Gaelic in Scotland since the time of James VI. He said that Gaelic was the principle cause of barbarity and incivility in his realm. He said the best thing was to stamp it out. And that was national policy until very recently. The damage has been done in people's minds.

The relationship between Gaelic and Scotland isn't nearly as simple ethnographically as the relationship between Welsh and Wales. The vast majority of Wales has been Welsh speaking, but in Scotland many languages have been spoken. To this day there's a big divide of Scots speakers, Gaelic speakers, and Scots-English speakers, so Gaelic isn't going to be the focus for national identity. And Scotland, unlike Wales and Ireland, has not been conquered. It still has its institutions— education, the church, the legal system – on which to base its identity. I don't think many people would look on Gaelic as a unifying identity for Scotland.

RK: *In one of your poems, 'Gaelic Concert' you describe a young person performing Gaelic on a stage in a city. Can Gaelic be performed anymore?*

MB: Probably with all art, it is best if an individual performer can point to universals. Maybe it is partly the amateurishness of some performances of Gaelic songs that projects a gauche individualism. With Gaelic songs in a traditional setting there was no distinction between participation and performance. The song wouldn't be any more the possession of the singer than of the listeners. The song would be considered a gift for the whole community, not a focus of admiration for the singer. I can think of a few singers who do sing traditional songs successfully on stage. It's usually the older ones who aren't so self-conscious, who you feel are a channel, a channel for the tradition, not an end in themselves.

RK: *What role does poetry have in preserving Gaelic?*

MB: It's not the job of poetry to preserve Gaelic. If it does preserve Gaelic in any way, it's a spin-off. When you write poetry your chief aim has to be the Muses. People living within the language, relating to one another, it is the only way for a language to survive. Gaelic singing and poetry are further down the line, and beyond that, education through the language, and way beyond that, Parliamentary documentation in Gaelic.

RK: *You were born in Edinburgh of English parents. Why study Gaelic?*

MB: The songs. I went to a concert in my early teens, and was bamboozled that there was such a different culture in my own country. The scale is pentatonic, and sounds quite different if you're used to the classical European eight point scale. I was amazed at the linguistic diversity of the country. There were romantic notions, too. I was drawn to the crofting lifestyle, to a non-technological way of life. There is something about the rigid class system in Edinburgh that always has got right up my nose.

I first went to university to do German and History of Art in Bristol, but was very homesick, then two years at Aberdeen in Celtic Studies. We weren't expected to become fluent. It was taught as a dead language. So I took a year out when other people doing modern languages were going to France and Germany. It wasn't heard of then to take a year off for Gaelic. It was an important year in lots of ways. There were seven children in the family, and I was like another one. I was working as an auxiliary nurse in a hospital run by nuns. I learned a lot more than Gaelic.

RK: *How does your poem 'Poetry Reading' fit in with this?*

MB: This poem arose when I was still in a very bad relationship, so the contrast between speaking to my partner and reading to a group was marked. You can feel not just distanced from the person you're meant to be closest to, but more comfortable in front of strangers, speaking almost as an abstract being. You feel yourself like a representative human being.

Some think I'm open about my life in my poems. I feel, *au contraire*, that I'm not, but I use the private details of my life only to extract universals. I never add a detail that doesn't also carry something symbolic. I try to get the double weight, a descriptive and a symbolic weight. I don't like poetry that only exposes the poet for the sake of exposing the poet. But maybe I've failed to, maybe I just think I'm trying to point towards universals, and in fact I'm being a blatant exhibitionist. A gratuitous exhibitionist!

Uan Marbh

Chan e a shròn a' sileadh fuil
air uchd mìn a tha mi a' caoidh,
no a' chaora ga shireadh
a-màireach 's an earar le ùthan làn,
no na mìosan a bha i ag at, a tòn
ris a' ghaoith, ris an uisge,
ri clachan meallain is sneachd.

Chan ann airson mar a sgrios mi an dealbh –
caora is uan nan laighe còmhla
madainn Chèitinn a' criomadh fhlùr –
le meatailt ghuineach Ford Fiesta
is brag mùchte,
is ise nist ga snòtaraich
le tuigse na cuinnleanan …

Tha mi caoidh mo thuigse fhèin
gun toir sinn dha na creutairean neochiontach
a bhriodeas, a spòthas, a rùisgeas, a spadas sinn,
ràithe sultmhorachd
as fhiach dhaibh a bhith beò.

Dead Lamb

It isn't its nose dropping blood
on its soft breast that I mourn,
or the ewe's seeking it out
tomorrow and the next day with distended udder,
or the months she was swelling, back end
to the wind, the rain,
to the hailstones and snow.

It isn't for the way I destroyed the idyll –
sheep and lamb lying together
on a May morning, nibbling flowers –
with wounding metal of Ford Fiesta
and a muffled thud,
the ewe now sniffing it,
an understanding in her nostrils …

I am mourning my own fond hope
that we can grant the innocent creatures
we breed, castrate, fleece and slaughter,
at least a season's well-being
that renders their existence worthwhile.

Leughadh Bàrdachd

Dh'fhàg mi aimhreit,
    dìth tuigse,
    droch-chàineadh
    aig an taigh.

Mi nist aig an deasg,
    làn cinnt
    gun tuigear nas fheàrr mi
    le srainnsearan.

Poetry Reading

I left discord,
    misconstruing,
    false accusations
    at home.

At the lectern now
    I'm certain
    I'll be better understood
    by strangers.

Ròs

Mo chridhe lom,
na caoin do ròs,
na caoin do bhlàthachadh
grad, corcra,
na caoin do bhileagan boga briste
a' tuiteam tè mu seach
gun fhios do dhuine.

Tha d' àilleachd na leug air bathais an òigeir,
tha do chùbhraidheachd na h-ortha ri uchd,
is fada bhuam
an gaol fhathast ga iadhadh,
ga phògadh le bilean buadhmhor eile.

Rose

My stripped heart,
don't weep for your rose,
don't weep for your blooming
sudden, crimson,
don't weep for your soft, broken petals
falling unnoticed, one by one.

Your beauty is a jewel on the young man's brow,
your fragrance a charm at his chest,
as far away love holds him still,
kissing him with other triumphant lips.

Mar Ròpa de Ghainmhich

le taing do Niall

Aon oidhche thàinig bualadh dhan doras
is grunn nàbaidhean a-staigh.
Nochd boireannach le pasgan na h-uchd.
Stad an còmhradh is i a' sgrùdadh na cuideachd.
"You're the faither. Ye can rear him".

Shàth i a h-eallach an uchd òigfhir
's thionndaidh i. Choimhead iad oirre
a' greasad sìos an lota dhan chladach.
Bha fireannaich ga feitheamh le geòla,
is bàta-iasgaich coimheach air acair sa bhàgh.

Chanadh iad Dodaidh ris.
Chaidh e na pheata aig a sheanmhair
is aig piuthar-athar is athair nach do phòs a-riamh.
Nuair a dh'fhàs e mòr bha e ainmeil airson a neirt
ach ghuil e mar phàist' nuair a fhuair a charaid bàs.

Dh'fhalbh iad uile is na bhuineadh dhaibh.
Dh'fhalbh an sgadan; tha an taigh-cèilidh na thobhta.
Chan eil fios dè na dualan de ghràdh 's de chràdh
– nis ma sgaoil mar ròpa de ghainmhich –
a cheangail rin càradh iad gun abhsadh.

Like a Rope of Sand

with thanks to Neil

One night a rapping came to the door
while the neighbours were gathered.
A woman stepped in, a bundle at her chest.
The talk stopped as she scoured the faces.
"You're the faither. Ye can rear him".

She thrust her burden at a young man
and was gone. They watched her
stride down the croft to the shore
where men were waiting with a dinghy.
A strange fishing boat lay at anchor in the bay.

They called the boy Dody,
the darling of his grandmother,
of his aunt and father. They never married.
And when he grew up he was famous for his strength,
but cried like a child when his friend was killed.

They are all gone, and those who belonged to them.
The herring are gone, the cèilidh house a ruin.
No-one remembers what strands of pain and passion
– unravelled now like a rope of sand –
bound them without slack to their history.

Tritheannan

Trì rudan air an leth-fhaicinn:
fàinne gorm mu shùil bodaich,
deàlradh na grèine tro thonn àrd,
bogha-frois ri solas na gealaich.

Trì rudan air an leth-chluinntinn:
duine a' crònan ri a phìob,
plaosgadh a' bhealaidh san Iuchar,
dòbhran a' dol fodha.

Trì rudan air an leth-fhaireachdainn:
bainne air anail laoigh,
an samhradh an leann flùir dromanaich,
sionnach sa choille.

Triads

Three things half-seen:
the blue rim round an old man's eye,

Meg Bateman, photograph by Domhnall Domhnallach

the sun glimpsed through a towering wave,
a rainbow by moonlight.

Three things half-heard:
a man humming to his pipes,
broom pods cracking in the heat,
an otter diving.

Three things half-smelled:
milk on a calf's breath,
the summer in elderflower beer,
a fox in the woods.

Sgàthan

Tha solas nan làithean ud
glacte ann an sgàthan m' inntinn,
mar sgàthan cruinn cam Van Eyck,
's tu fhèin 's mi fhìn ann,
gun dùrd, gun ghluasad,
mo làmh aig cùl do chinn
's do làmh-sa air mo chliathaich
san deàlradh shòlaimte ud;
tha sgleò air a' chòrr de na làithean
is air na mìosan bhon uair sin,
's sinn ann an glacaibh a chèile
ann am boillsgeadh geal na cuimhne,
an sgàthan mì-fhreagarrach làn
san dorchadas a tha gar n-iadhadh.

Mirror

All the light of those few days
is held in the mirror of my mind
like that curved mirror of Van Eyck's,
you and me reflected in it,
wordless, unmoving,
my hand at the back of your head,
your hand on my side,
in that solemn luminosity,
the rest of the days irrelevant
and intervening months,
us holding each other still
in the unchanging light of memory,
the mirror incongruously full
amid the surrounding darkness.

Note: the last three poems will appear in *Soirbheas/Fair Wind,* forthcoming from Birlinn.

Charlie Gracie

right

We must strive to build a culture of life – George W Bush

a one thousand pound Tomahawk Cruise missile
slices the sky above the Persian Gulf

scales the blue hypnotic sea
into the ancient spread of desert
tilting over the soft rises of the land
a blur of steel

bears down in forty-four minutes on Baghdad
as it sleeps
on the snaky tail of the Tigris

glides into the city like an owl
quiet and secretive
till it sears through the walls
of Zubaida's house
she in her room
her child in her womb
his thumb in his mouth
all quiet and tucked up
in amniotic safety

we talked about love at the end of the earth

we stood there
on the wild loud edge of the sea
on black pitted rock

waves crashed
from the cliffed edge of the land
stretched high into the space between
heaven and earth
clawed at the clouds in a wet rage

I tasted salt in the air
like my own blood

I said it was vehemence
that spilled from the waves
as they spat their froth to the sky
vehemence that roared
deep from the belly of the sea

I think the land is waiting, you said
for the waves to still
to soften the crags
and whisper into the cracked earth
and sleep
cooried in

sparkling

towards Dachau
you all slept
not taking in
the fields rising and falling
with barley in its last weeks of goldening
nor the spired church tilting above the houses
nor the biz of the autobahn whirring
nor the europop spilling from the speakers

as we swept past the slip road
I took a drink of water
from the plastic bottle
eased the rim to my mouth
felt the sparkle of mineral water
on my tongue
shooshing in my throat

they call it prickelnd in German

a sparkle prickling my throat

I screwed the lid tight
and drove on

dirty wee smack heid

on waste ground
against a tree
on the edge of budding
you were found

just beyond the railway bridge
among broken glass
here daffodils hang their heads

(they say you had your eyes wide open)

flowers
your mother left
a card
for a special son

Old Mrs Morse's Door

An Excerpt from Ramshackle, *a Novel*

Elizabeth Reeder

Roe Davis, plain old fifteen, wakes up one Saturday morning and finds her dad's gone missing. He's taken his shoes, coat, hat and gloves. It's January in the middle of a bitter Chicago winter and wherever he is, he'll be cold.

It's Tuesday and Roe and her Aunt Linden have just reported her dad missing. At home, life is fraught, but quiet, as she tries to find clues as to why he's left. But at school, no one knows her dad's missing and there's nothing she can do but get on with life as she knows it.

"I've been thinking about beauty and grace," Mr R says. He's sitting at his desk, twirling his beard. His beard that's in need of a trim. Before she left him, I bet his wife used to sit him down in a chair and trim his beard without her top on. Heavy hanging breasts brushing his chin.

"What about truth?" asks Missy.

"No Keats today," he says. "Truth is too elusive to speak of here."

"Today, we're going to talk about spiders." He flicks off the lights, turns on a video, some nature program he's taped off National Geographic or something. It's on mute, so he can narrate. "See how she moves? Their lovemaking is quick, slightly clumsy at that.' Most everyone shifts in their seats at the mention of sex, but he doesn't notice. "But when she devours him, it's all grace and beauty. Deadly, for a minute, chaos, followed by calm."

"Unless she'd already eaten lunch!" Freddie shouts.

Violent departure and then silence.

"I want you to write about a movement of beauty that ends in silence."

And I want to write about my dad and how he walks, and how the apron straps hang down his back when he cooks, or his smock straps when he works, how he's a fortress, so concentrated and intense and how I'm not there at all in his head or his movements, and yet watching him, over the top of a book or magazine, are moments when he and I are closest. Beauty. Silence.

"Where do you think you're going, Miss Davis?" Mr Pavich's voice is steel sharp, his eyes bore into my back.

"To my seat." I continue to walk up the aisle.

"Stop!"

I stop but don't turn around.

"Where is your signed test?"

"I forgot."

"Then you're not welcome in my class. Go to the principal's office."

It's on principle he's sending me to the principal, because the principal is my pal.

"I can get it for you tomorrow." My desk is inches away. If I could just sit down, I'll become invisible, he'll leave me alone.

"Not good enough. Go now. Before I give you detentions."

I'm hot. I want to slap my hands down on his desk and head-butt him. If it didn't mean my forehead would get all greasy. He's either producing slime or he slaps so much grease on to keep his comb-over in place.

"That's not fair." It's Jess speaking up for me. My heart soars.

"Do you think it was fair when the Serbs stole land from the Croats? When they put them in camps? Raped and murdered them? Was that fair?" We had to force him into it, but he finally did a bit of actual teaching. He even has a point, but it doesn't mean a thing coming from his mouth. Not enough.

"Outta here," is all I manage before pushing the door when it should be pulled. My classmates erupt in laughter behind me. I run my hand over rows and rows of lockers. My hand bouncing out every time I hit the lock and small pull handle. I take my time.

Someone's opened the window in the principal's office. A wave of frigidity cuts through the room. Miss Stevenson, the secretary stares me down like I'm Hitler or something. It was only a test. A stupid test. Who cares? Mrs Melbourne looks at me kindly, my record till now is impeccable and she lets me off with a warning and a note to get back into class.

Mr Pavich has pinned up all of our maps and they dangle there from the cork rail that rims the room. They flap in some random draft. I put the note on the table. Mr Creep turns around and rubs his stubby hands together. Picks at his nails, which even I can see are yellowing. Hope he's close to some major illness. Or death.

He hurls dates and names at us, assumed battles, dragging us across vast distances and times, back and forth between countries and alliances. I feel dizzy and sick. My map sits over his right shoulder and looks like a cauliflower growing out of his ear.

He concludes in the middle of some country's civil war. My notebook is full up with notes. "One by one I want you to go up to your map and write the grade you think you deserve on it. And tell us why." There's a thick black marker we each need to use. Jess is first. As always. She picks up the pen from off the desk and swings her hips up to her map.

"I should get an A," Jess says. "Because it's stunning and correct. See this bit of coast here? You'll notice the dual shades because for sixteen days in May 1943 it fell into enemy hands before being reclaimed."

My best friend the suck-up.

I'm last, his system for hanging these horrible things, crystal clear. From the left side of his head, round the room, down the grade-scale, to my cauliflower. The little shit. I'm really calm to start with but then my heart beats and beats. I have something important to say, but don't know how to say it, when to say it. How to make a controversial point.

"I should get a C," I say, after Veronica Sampson hands me the pen. Her D, clear and defeated on her map. She just one of many, like the entire rest of the class willing to put themselves down in public. Life's too short to be a good girl. I write a big black 'C' on my map. "Because I've worked really hard, I've listened to the scant information actually taught in class, I tape record the class, listen to it later, with a map in front of me, have forty pages of notes for this term alone. I'm smart too. I think my map is less perfect than it should be because," and this is where I know I step over a line, "the teaching sucks."

He says nothing. Goes with his smug red pen and over the front of each map he scrawls our grades. Jess gets a B, as punishment for standing up for me, even though her map is first up on the wall and a couple of A- scores follow hers. And her perfect map is ruined. He moves around the vicious circle, on down the scale until mine.

"And this is a perfect detail of an amoeba Miss Davis," and he writes an easy 'F' and his hand hovers and he finishes with a flourish: '–'. The bell rings.

Another made up grade. Made up for maximum public humiliation.

"Well done Colonel Pavich," I say, straddling the door between a slow death and freedom. I start to clap my hands, "You've created a dictatorship." I hope my dad comes home tonight so I never ever have to come back to this class.

"You're in the shit now," Jess laughs.

"Sorry he punished you too."

"Down with Hitler," she says. Then she opens her mouth wide and mocks teeth being pulled out. "Speaking of which, have a great time at the dentist."

I don't have a note for this either. Too bad.

"See ya later." I say and run to my locker, put my hands out to protect myself from all the crap that threatens to fall. Grab my coat, shove more stuff in and walk calmly through the exit least likely to be watched over.

The bus rides low and slow to the station and I start here with the end of the line: Linden (an aunt, a tree, a train station). Any journey I take on these trains starts or ends with family. Starts and ends with family. Travels through family too. Is this what fate has in for me? That I pass through, these people who have adopted me, every time I try to get home? Or leave home? Is that what life has in store for me?

It's the first or last station on the Purple Line, with a platform enclosed on three sides; I sit on the train and wait for us to move. The heat isn't on yet and I'm frozen despite my long underwear and my coat which reaches my thighs and the hat which everyone tells me will keep in the heat but only makes my head itch.

Doors closing.

Welcome to Purple Line run 511.

Central is next.

In the direction of travel, doors open on the left at Central.

The announcements are on some sort of personalized loop. A male voice, metallicised as it works its way through the system and out the speakers. The Metra train, the posh train, passes through Central too, a few blocks west. And at Davis, two more stops on, (*doors open on the right at Davis*) the Metra is close enough to touch. We used to get off at Davis to go to our dentist on Church Street. Now I get off at Dempster, because it's closer to the high rise building he's in now, that smells like rubber.

I get off the train. Visit the third generation dentist so young I can't believe he's out of high school. He must be. I've got one cavity at the back, have to go back next week. I say no to the whitening option.

Back at the station. The pigeon-shit makes the platform sticky. Humans fight for space with the birds beneath the heater.

My dad and I must be the only people on the north shore who use the train regularly, who don't drive everywhere.

"Your grandpa was a fanatic," my dad says, as though he's any different, "I just like to ride the 'L' for the joy of it. It's a habit."

"It's an obsession, Dad."

"Maybe."

And Peter Berwyn Davis doesn't care. He pushes kids and elderly women out the way to get the first seat on the train, up by the driver.

"The first real view of the city is just before you hit Howard." All change at Howard. "The Hancock comes into view. Right there." My dad always points straight ahead, as if he was in the front car. "Best seats in the house." He says of the front, "I often have to sit next to the professional train riders, smelling of groin sweat."

"Oh, Dad, that's too much information."

"But it's true," he says. "Mustier than armpit sweat, which is there too. And old piss. The piss is on the floor and I always think that it's awfully mean because the drivers are right there, and some guys just whip it out and take a pee on the floor."

"Dad!"

"Don't be such a girl. A body is a body is a body."

"But it's gross."

"Maybe a bit. But that's life. Remember the time you knocked out your front teeth?"

"Of course."

"It hurt right?"

"You bet. And gross too."

"Well, it's like that. Blood and guts and pain. It may not be pretty, but it's real."

"And why is that better?"

"Because you know you're alive."

Between our house and Old Mrs Morse's a stalker's path foot-cuts down the ravine to a small cove of sand. It's not wide but it stretches further towards the water than it used to, although the lake has crowded in a bit more in recent years. It's a private beach and teenagers go down there drinking all the time. It used to be that if Old Mrs Morse liked them (like if they left cold beer on her porch) she'd let them alone, but if they took a leak in her forsythia or her roses she'd call the cops.

Our beach comes in and out of fashion. Some years we have weekend after weekend of partying, barbaric yawps, of bonfires, of couples arguing outside my window. One year a car didn't stop at the end of the road and went over the ravine.

I barely remember it. It ploughed between our houses, went right through and out into the air like a cartoon car with no road under it and over the edge, taking one of the oldest maples with it. The driver, a girl, drunk, and only just a handful of days past sixteen, died when the steering went right through her body, and the driver's seat, and ended up in the backseat.

Old Mrs Morse was furious about the tree. Everyone else said what a shame about the girl. "Just stupid," Mrs Morse said. "Just stupid. She knew the risks. She took them. I hear she fought for the damn car keys. A dumb kid. The world is a safer place without her."

The skid marks started half way down the street and turned into deep welts in the mud just before the edge.

"We have no idea how she got up the speed to do it."

"I'm telling you," Old Mrs Morse would say, "it was suicide."

A big crane came and pulled up the car. The water was way back by then and the car wasn't even wet. Its bumper was wrapped around the tree it'd hit and there were branches stuck out of the windows, sand falling from its front fender.

I always wondered about the girl. Was she stupid? Or did she know exactly what she was doing?

When I get home from the dentist's, Mrs Morse's house is alive with sunlight. It bounds off the windows, throughout the house. The big space inside is reeling with the light. Even without her inside, her grey braid swinging, her old strong frame, it's still hers.

Dad and I had tried to put it into some order but we'd not put in the time. A few bags of clothes to the Salvation Army and that's about it. Her year of absence, and every time I'm inside all I can think is about how it smells of her.

It is hers.

In the last few days in her house, the water tormented Old Mrs Morse, with the heavy waves crashing in the dark, the roots of the trees creaking, pulling at the house. I stayed with her a few nights, joined her while she paced and ranted. I put out my arm and she hooked her own through it. Her thin white nightdress. And a thick robe, must have been her husband's, I wrapped her in, and she was warmer but smelled musty and looked more senile. And I was sorry I'd done it. I try not to have that image of her when I think of her, try not to remember her calling me Peter, because I want to believe that the Village killed her when they sent her away to the old folks' home, when she could have taken care of herself. But those nights, I wasn't sure which I found more frightening, the roaring of the lake, or her own ranting.

To live in fear of what might happen. She'd been living with small fears for years. But near the end, the fear took over, even though the lake wasn't going to take her house this time, in the middle of the night you could never be sure.

I always thought that I'd be the first one to leave. Both of us were fools.

Mrs Morse drove a "74 pea green Ford station wagon, with fake wood runners, and rust like a fringe along the bottom and at all the joints, a tank of a thing as people moved from station wagons to mini-vans and SUVs, and then Hummers.

"They're stumped, aggressive things," Mrs Morse used to say. Eventually, she downsized to a bike.

She wore her long black hair braided, usually just a single braid, but sometimes tucked up inside a hat, if she'd been gardening; she'd held onto her beauty like other older people had not.

"It's this house," she'd say, "it keeps me young. There's magic at the door when you step through. My dad built it that way."

"The Village wants this land," she'd say, "and I'd half give it, if it didn't mean giving up this house."

I always used to play along the shore with the rest of the kids, wading with my trousers turned up. It was my hatred of the water that felt like lead in the ball and socket of my hip. Not the idea of water, not water from a distance, but the sand-grit reality of it. The inconvenience. The unpredictability. Hatred, not fear. Like me with mad Pavich. The hatred of water is part of me. I used to go down to the cove, faking interest when Dad was there. But when I went alone I scooted timid, on my butt, over the rocks, down the dirt slide. I picked my way among the rubble of the house, mixed with the, detritus of Milwaukee's trash. The breaker rocks were supposed to stop more erosion and I guess they were doing their job even as used condoms and maxi-pads got stuck in the deep crevices carved out as the water advanced and receded with the rain.

I never go down to the water like this. Not alone, not with the dark falling fast. The ice as thick as I've ever seen it. The moon thin as I've ever seen it. The city glows red to the south, and somehow, from somewhere, there's light. There's a crack, but nothing moves. I've never known a place so quiet. I walk up the steep embankment and to her house.

These days I'm afraid. I admit it. I have keys, one of which must be hers. When she was alive I could go over any time and her back door would be unlocked. But now, since she died, dad kept her keys. Last year, at the beginning of spring, the Village put up bright police tape to keep people out, like it was the scene of a crime, a murder. My dad ripped it down soon as they'd gone.

"We don't need to advertise that it's empty."

Don't need to advertise that it will be brought low. The winter shadow of the house spills down the ravine. Its plunge is sudden, unbearable. I couldn't find the flashlight and grab dad's headlamp instead, the one he wears to Mrs Morse's when he's working over there.

No new snow since Sunday night. It's all crystal and crunches beneath my boots. I used to walk on snow like this, its crusty top sometimes an inch thick. And me, light on my feet, walking across, above the ground.

"I'm walking on water!" I'd yell. Me, thinking myself clever.

The crust breaks again and again. With each step.

I zigzag my feet to find the safest spaces on the stairs. The wood planks, once sealed and painted a steel grey blue, have buckled and look sickly flesh-like between the cracked paint. The steps run parallel to the house, the planks of the porch come out at perpendicular and you can see the rough convex bits where water has buckled the wood. Splinters in your feet in the summer. Slippery covered in ice. I put my arms out to the side for balance.

The door is locked. I don't need to try the handle to know it.

The de-icer clanks in my pocket, against her keys. Of course I'll have to use it. Acrid, harsh fumes flit up my nose and freeze there. I have a feeling I'll wake up in the middle of the night, smelling like a factory. Smelling more than a bit like Linden.

I spray some de-icer on the keys, on the single lock on Old Mrs Morse's front door and I wonder how she got away with that, living next door to my dad for so long. But she did. I have at least ten possible keys, on different rings. Although hers will be a triple set of keys, only one of her locks will be locked. That's the key I'm after. Some I can clearly disregard out of hand. Lever keys when this is a simple pin-tumbler Yale. All the keys are copies, so they don't really match the feel of the lock.

The door would be easy to kick in, but it's on principle that I go through key after key. I wouldn't be my dad's daughter if I resorted to force. The key that finally works is a rough fit. A bad copy, years old. I wonder if my dad's other copy is better because this one's a travesty.

I've not been in this house for months and as the door swings open, creaks on winter hinges, it's still like death in there.

My toes remain outside, on the door-stop, and I pull my hand back. The last of the day's light slants weakly through the house from west to east, dark racing on its heels.

I step through, into her house, for the first time since my dad left. I am looking for something. A reason maybe, although an answer would be better. The keys are heavy in my pocket, the space of the house open before me. The house is still, arctic.

I take out my headlamp. It makes the world even stranger. All the peripheral information is lost. Light to pitch to lost.

I turn from side to side, light sweeping like a lighthouse. Must look creepy from outside but no one will be watching.

I don't know where to begin. Don't know where to look. What am I looking for? Things lost? Things to be lost? Precarious or precious. Solid or safe? This house is anything but abandoned. If anything it's been loved too much, if that's possible. With everything Mrs Morse had to give and Dad too.

And now it's waiting for them to come back. And no one else will do.

I stand in the hall. The stairs straight ahead, the living room to the right, the dining room that leads to the kitchen to the left. I head towards the kitchen. Start with the familiar. Not one to waste space, she built a bookcase beneath the stairs. Jammed it not with books, but with stuff. Dusty, slightly damp stuff. The dust has become dirt and what had once been cleanly delineated sheets of paper has paper-machied into paper pulp.

We've never cleaned the house. It's part of why I feel bad. I should have felt bad about all of this well before now. Totally bad. Curl up in a ball bad about losing Mrs Morse. Instead we just left it all to rot.

The house smells like her. Earth right up from the foundation, her gardening gloves still flopped over a nail near the back door, the frame a grey-blue, well-weathered, cracked and chipped. Her kitchen counters are wide appliance-free expanses, her fridge is in our house now, cranking away. No power here any more. A shovel rests by the back door. When she was taken away, dad and I bundled her plants over to our house and they died within a month. Maybe the move, maybe grief.

Years and years ago, the lake left a rent in the wall at the back. Thick builders' plastic covered the opening for a long time. "Too long for it to be right," Dad said. "Years longer than was right."

"Throwing up that damn wall was admitting defeat," she said for ages after, "That stupid lake had won again."

The wall does the job it's supposed to do. More window than brick, as any lake facing wall should be. The two parts of the house were supposed to work together, flow, and it wasn't just that the house was slightly old, that it was running down the hill towards dilapidation, it was that it hadn't been whole for years.

"You need to remember where you've come from," Dad said. "I built that with my own hands. Remember that. These frivolous, key-cutting hands built that. And it matters."

I'm remembering so much that it hurts. The dust on all the surfaces is untouched. The door stuck in the middle of the living room, aloof. I try to imagine what my dad has touched in this house. How did this house touch him? What made him love this place? And love Mrs Morse?

I used to play hide and seek here all the time. Open and close the old door that she'd mounted right in the middle of her living room, frame and all. I'd step through into another world. Shouting to Mrs Morse to play a king or a princess or a queen bee. And she would, she'd step through into my world, raise and lower her voice, crink her fingers.

I run my gloved hands up part of the frame, across the bevelled surface, to the handle. I look closely, rust clings to the edges of the lock, which looks tight and strong, even unlocked as it is. I can't bring myself to turn the handle. I need it to open easily. To stay intact. I need WD40.

Down in the basement the cobwebs are peaceful. Older than a year old. Decades old. A workbench, with hammers hanging from makeshift holds, big drawers with metal crescent handles, plastic containers with tiny drawers for all sorts of nails and screws and fittings.

Chandeliers of cobwebs decorate the ceiling and what looks to be an abandoned wasps' nest hugs a corner by the outer wall. Mrs Morse wasn't a dress-up sort of grandmotherly type. She was a 'let's thin out this jungle that my back yard has become' type and hand you an axe or a shovel. "Let's paint this." "Cut this down." "Plant this."

I see how she seduced my dad: with fresh air, hard work and a mile of her father's tools down in the basement.

The headlamp flickers, I hit it with my hand, and it goes out completely. There's just enough light from outside to outline the door. I'm up the stairs in a flash and then I'm outside Mrs Morse's house with pitch black space behind me. I look at the lights next door, coming from our house. The windows lit up bright like a face. I don't know what I was thinking, it's the opposite of a beacon. It's garish. Intrusive.

Who would want to go back there? Inside our house the answering machine light flashes. Two messages. My heart in my throat. I trail snow and cold across the room. Press the button. The first message is from Officer Berg who says that my dad's credit card has been used down in Champaign. Does he know anyone there? she asks.

Then Mr Pavich's voice cracks from the machine. How'd he get our number?

"Mr Davis, we need to talk about your daughter's appalling performance in my class. And her attitude. I know you're a reasonable man, Mr Davis. Keep her on a tighter lease or you'll end up with an unwanted pregnancy. Mark my words. I've seen this thing before. Make sure she studies for tomorrow's test. Where will she be without history? She'll be cursed to repeat it. Anything less than a C and she'll flunk the class."

I'm gonna flunk the creep's class.

Norman Kreitman

The Big Names

Saturdays in winter could be trusted.
Queue up at the Classic, and for six pence
you got not only Laurel and Hardy
but five more shorts, so for an afternoon
clutched a roller-coaster
of convulsing giggles and dread suspense.

But first came the manager, glowering
through the smell of sweat and tangerine,
prowling the gangway and shaking a cane
at the bedlam of urchins, though everyone knew
his only hope of winning
was when Flash Gordon whizzed across the screen.

Deliciously the others followed. A custard pie
unerringly covered the courteous Chaplin smile.
Villains collapsed in the order required
for the vindication of modest heroes --
Tom Mix of the smoking gun,
Tarzan, who weekly slaughtered a crocodile.

At the interval from a magic pit
all shimmering in gold and electric stars
climbed the Wurlitzer, and in its light
the Merry Widow waltz danced round
the scalloped, peachy curtains.
Blasé, you leaned back and chewed your Mars.

Then again the arms of darkness wrapped you warm.
The screams that greeted Goofy shook the roof,
but to bring a firmer order to the shifting world
came the intellectual prowess and urbanity
of subtle Charlie Chan,
for Eastern proverbs always lead to truth.

The weeks were phrased in years, until
each big name gave way to a bigger player
who acted in larger, more orderly houses.
Yet you cannot relax, for all their fame,
with comic Time, who blunders,
or Mr. Death, the great betrayer.

Geoffrey of Dryburgh

We could make nothing of him, Lord, that wild
gesticulating stranger, with his babble in some barbaric tongue;
so we bathed him, gave him meat, pointed him firmly
towards Melrose.

Twilight now; the birds are beginning to call
across the garden, the trees to commune in the autumn breeze.
I sit in my small, damp cell, dutiful, reciting Vespers by rote.

But sometimes on a wordless prayer
my spirit slips through the grille, gropes its way skywards
to find You. And sometimes – but these days, oh so rarely –

I think You speak to me, only to find
it is my own voice returning. As I see those trees
only as my eyes allow, hear only as the ear permits, so my mind

is the prisoner of language,
and I am confounded by paradox and metaphors.
This I must endure. But Lord, I grow so weary of Your silence

who am that stranger You send stumbling on his way.

Another Sussex Church

So there it was, yet another Sussex church,
benign as a huddle of sheep, the nave as white,
the pews ordered like generations, and a vault

to collect the musings of bored congregations
while sermons dragged their endless proprieties.
A window, diamonds of crimson and blue

nudged my attention, and I paused to admire
the pace of the mullions, approve the weave
of stone arching through the Jesse tree.

But a feeble interest in English Perpendicular
did not assuage a sense of trespassing
(I went in to avoid the February weather).

Then suddenly I saw through a clear pane
a scarecrow crucified upon the skyline,
coat-tails streaming in the cruel wind.

But that shock of the primitive found relief
in two jars of dispirited snowdrops under 'Hymn 24',
card bookmarks by the Women's Guild, priced 20p.

Tranquillised by the mundane I felt consoled,
could ask "What else did you expect?"
and like any rational man went back into the rain.

The Devils

No tree, no stone is free of them.
A hundred may swarm in a teacup
though one alone could fill the temple hall.
They swirl in legions over village rooftops
hunting a single crack -- an improper thought,
some careless word, an unconsidered gesture –
        to penetrate, and seize.

You will know the possessed by their ravenous hunger,
their predatory eyes. Puppets now, they twitch
when they walk, jerked by the laughing devils -
O to feel with hands, to smell the scent of leather!
For just one hour in the warmth of human skin
those transparent ones would gladly die,
        if death were possible.

And only the shaman's fiercest mantra
can bludgeon them into exile, send them back
into the wind and its wild despair
as it screams through the Himalayan peaks
or sinks in desolate, empty alleys.
All you who neglect the body's beneficence
        consider well the ghosts of Tibet.

Julie-ann Rowell

An Struibh Broín

I dip my hand into the water
and feel the cool glide of *An Struibh Broín*

the tickle of the undercurrent
where stones might be hearts.

It's said if you drink from this river
it will ease the agony of going to sea.

A cure-all for the heart is a common thing,
but I wonder at the moss soft as hair,

any power of belief as men set sail
into unbelievable winds,

their eyes like the pale river,
their hopes receding as the land recedes,

a face in mind, imprinted like a birthmark,
as real, as obvious. Many things can be erased

but not this. They will pull on their ropes
to forget and turn into the sorry waves.

Returning from Toraigh

Home to the Country as the islanders called it,
and on the boat is a man with a club foot,
talipes equinovarus, he wears a surgical boot
to compensate. I haven't seen the like of in years

that physical division, now correctable at birth.
We're so defined by the body, as the Island
is by the weather, these squally interruptions,
the beating of the Sound we cross uneasily.

The sky's full of gannets, their wingtips dipped in ink,
and razorbills skim the swell. The boat is lifted
and pulled. We are always leaving something,
a place, a heart. How sturdy they must be

these islanders. These Toraigh people. I want
to shelter amongst their granite, against the silver rain,
the sudden dips and turns of the sea. Take what it means
to be me and plant it in their earth.

A Middle-aged Woman Faints in Preservation Hall

They carried her out into Bourbon Street
where a small boy waited, studying the moment
as if he knew her – a psychic might
have insisted on a previous life.
They advertised aplenty, the 'Nawlin's'
palm readers, clairvoyants, but she
did not believe in second chances.
The pavement felt so solid unlike
inside where it was as if the jazz
could lift her to the ceiling. The new air
was tight. She'd been propped
amongst cigarette ends and plastic cups.
The small boy held out his hand to her, but
she did not want to be touched.

Cygnus Cygnus

It's when I lie down at night I think
of the whooper swans at the tundra lake
lying in the tall grasses, and how they sleep –
the thought of a wild thing sleeping. You said
they visit from Iceland for the summer,
the kind of detail you would know, and share.
It stills me to imagine their eyes closed,
no matter if it's a starry night. No matter
if the moon sits on the water. No matter
that clouds might interrupt. No matter.

The St Louis Cemetery

The dead lie above ground in this mad heat.
I wander through their little streets while
beseeching angels watch, and others close
their eyes amongst the plastic tokens, photographs.
Flowers don't last long here.

Six generations in one tomb, joined forever
in bonds I can never share down to the last link
with recent home. A flow of hearts: a daughter's
to a father's to a wife's. I like to think I am seen;
that we are children amongst the white stones,
the entreaties, the prayers. Baffled as ever
by such a place; lost in the small town maze.

Evening

The evening gathers itself
for the full-on night.

I am at the walnut tree
which is ripening itself

in my friend's garden,
in the arms of a mood

for the thing gone. Lost.
I can't even express

this wandering. It isn't
you, though it could be.

It's just happenstance,
the moon's ring,

the idea of a halo,
a whisper in the grass.

The Beckoning Sun

Robert Ewing

Granted, I am not the most slender specimen.

I am stout. My jowls quiver when I turn my head. I catch sight of my face in a mirror on the wall opposite and it gives me pause. That odd person, there: holding the coffee cup under an impossibly lumpen face, pale and hairless. (We will disregard my hairlessness for now: suffice it to say that the hairy areas are there to prevent the skin of vulnerable organs gluing together.) I must present a curious figure altogether: bald, stout, pale0skinned. A drunken enemy at University once likened me to a flat fish in a cave: round, damp to the touch, and colourless. It's only now, with my new found confidence, that I can admit the description was apt.

Sunshine does not agree with me. But frivolous Swedish cakes most certainly do: they fill the plate in front of me and I gorge and wilt. I attack them with my spoon. *Princess torta. Success torta. Mazarine torta.* And most especially, *biscvir* and *fragilite* – melting sensations in the mouth.The newspaper flutters in my hands, an espresso within reach, the steady murmur of others enjoying this new *Konditori*. A sublime moment! Chocolate flecks the corners of my mouth; I dab it with a crisp square of linen.

Now you know how I look. So it might surprise you to know what I do for a living. My profession's not a comfort zone for the overweight. It is not a safe haven. My colleagues are not the most, shall we say, understanding of one's foibles.

I am a doctor. A family practitioner. *Ah.* Now you see the problem. Perhaps you are already there, constructing the unedifying scenes, the daily difficulties. Beads of sweat betraying one during close examinations. The hands perpetually damp. Trousers sailing low on the backside while bending over. Face flustered when a cool, unruffled exterior is called for.

Being hot and bothered and, God forbid, imperfect.

Of course it all comes down to diet. I know this. And of course, so do my patients. My face stiffens with mortification each time I'm forced to tiptoe around the subject. They press me on it, sometimes cruelly. They'll ask: *Can you think of anything else I might be doing wrong, doctor?* I'll hesitate, caught. *Erm ... sensible pursuits, that's the ticket.* They'll smile and say, *But anything else you can think of? Nothing obvious?* I start to blather, finger worrying at my collar: *Not too much to drink ... although a little red wine now and then will do you no harm.*

I cannot be cruel. It's not just a matter of being large and losing the moral high ground when it comes to lifestyle counselling. I'm just not in it for being cruel, for delivering the foul medicine. I'm a sensitive soul. I flatter myself to say that I'm a good doctor, a passable practitioner: not too much emotional blackmail (you'll have gathered), a little compassion, a few

Illustration by Shona Dougall

liberal spoonfuls of sympathy, and a lot of listening. And a bit of advice too, I suppose. *A big fat pushover,* I might have said, before it happened.

But – and now we come to what I've been building up to tell you – it all made me sick. I burned out. I had every feature they describe in the books. I was depersonalised. Unproductive. No concentration. Irritable. Depressed. I made mistakes. Terrible mistakes.

I was perpetually tired, but I couldn't sleep. I somatised freely: developed bizarre migrating kidneys and non-existent stomach masses and the persistent sensation of a lump in my throat. I had a series of disastrous (and frankly non-consensual) relationships. I dabbled with sedatives, rather more excessively, with alcohol.

I shouldn't really blame the relationship I had with my patients, but in truth I was always too proximate. To their lives. I was always reaching for the tissues, often prematurely. I have a friend, a psychiatrist who had an abusive, alcoholic father. She described him once as *emotionally unavailable*. But I was the opposite – emotionally *over-available*. Over involved. I gave out my telephone number, and they would phone up and snuffle at me in the middle of the night. I became a machine for offering solace, began to feel like a funeral clerk after an outrage: word had got out. And the word was: *the big fellow listens.* Families would attend with their collective woes. My surgeries ran three hours over. And it nearly killed me.

I suppose self-preservation kicked in. After a night spent staring at a bottle of pills I made efforts to repair myself. A holiday in Venice with a girl-friend, cutting out the drink, the tablets, hypnotherapy, meditation.

But I was slipping away, falling into a well and seeing daylight recede – there's a clunky image!. But it felt just so: I was disappearing. Despite my planetary mass, I was sliding between the cracks. Chocolate kept me sane. But the demand on the cocoa-producing nations of this world was unsustainable. My heart and my trousers complained. My bladder wept.

And so, just before I disappeared completely, it happened.

I had my epiphany. When I was at school, I always wanted to have an epiphany. The word meant a lot. It had its religious connotations, and it held the promise of transformation. I would write it out in fine lettering on the inside of my jotters. It looked so cool: so *Holden Caulfield*.

But it never happened. I began to hate Holden and Salinger when I decided that epiphanies were for other kids: slender kids like Holden with the chutzpah to rebel in an adult world. Epiphanies were not for rotund, shy, inadequate bookworms. So I fell to affected cynicism. I could be heard in corridors proclaiming who would listen, to those even more put upon than I – *if you know what an epiphany is, then you won't get one.*

But I did. It happened.

In the beginning it was such an ordinary moment. Morning surgery. A mother and her infant child in the consulting room with me. I was kneeling, examining the child. The usual tightness in my chest, my heart beating as if set in concrete, my shirt waterlogged. The mother talking to me, but I wasn't listening. The child had a sticky film over its eyes – viral conjunctivitis and an upper respiratory tract infection (when will doctors learn that brevity is better than verbosity?) I had already written out a prescription, and my routine explanation was there in mind forming at the pace of a typesetter setting out a page. Then it happened.

I looked at the child, and the child looked so *pampered*. So cared for. Its every need, its every limbic urge or bodily function taken care of. I stared at the child, and realised that I was doing so, but I couldn't stop myself, because I was so grateful. I thought: *this child is the key.* I wanted to weep, and was transported back to my first communion: kneeling at the altar, nauseous with excitement with the wafer in my mouth. Smells of incense and lacquer and polished floor. Then looking up from the priest and seeing over his head a painting of Mary, wearing her blue mantle and supporting the Christ child. I remember being so very moved by the icon.

Back in the surgery, I wept. The poor woman left in a hurry with her child as I broke down on my desk blotter. The staff and the other partners were very kind; they picked up, rescheduled my appointments.

I left work early, and went home to sleep.

I awoke, and a lightness had returned. I had much to do. So much to do, when I think about it now. First, the living room. I pulled up the carpet, and with a marker pen, drew a rough circle over the uncovered boards. Seeing what I had done, my heart skipped, quite painlessly.

I took the rest of the week off work. At a £150 pounds call out charge I had a carpenter (a rather baffled fellow) cut through the floorboards. Then I commissioned a labourer and his gang to dig a hole for me, to a depth of six feet, rerouting pipes and electricity cables.

The next day was Saturday. Three brisk gentlemen in green overalls arrived from Smiley's Jacuzzi and flotarium installations. They raised eyebrows at my unorthodox request, but I was steadfast, and they set to business. I left them to it and went shopping. When I returned, the living-room was a sensation. I was trembling with anticipation; tears filled my eyes. So desperate was I to get the men out that I rudely brushed off their introduction to the apparatus, proffering twenty pound notes just to be rid of them. Finally, they left me alone. I filled the sump with water, and turned the thermostat to a steady 37. The room filled up with silken fog, a joyful mist. My first night was a revelation, a discovery of self. My skin was wrinkled and sheeting when I repaired to bed in the wee small hours.

And so we are here. And it gets better and better. Each night better than the last. When I come home the room is filled with candles. Roses delivered to the door. The words of an admirer: me. I buy large cotton towels. I have learned to plait these the old fashioned way. They never unfold or unfurl. I have safety pins made out of gold.

Now I can see that it makes sense for me to be hairless. And once the mirrors are in place, my gaze will be complete. The compressor and scuba diving apparatus, with a little practice, will take me further still.

I have a lady who sees to my needs. The business of setting things right. As Swift would have it: my *disburthenments*. She is a jolly soul, unimpeachable in her work. She wears latex gloves and has dimples on her cheeks, and a curling forelock appearing under her white hat, always perfectly in place. She sees to my difficult, irregular functions. Her finger is quite as dexterous as a hummingbird's tongue.

Now I have distance. I try not to get too involved. I tell my patients, who try to reach me in their old ways, who try to push their problems and their cares over to me: find out what makes you happy. For the twenty-first century blues, you are on your own. Go find your own happiness.

I can be flippant with them sometimes.

And so we are here, in this fine new *Konditori*. And do you know, I'm already at home. You're talking to me, and I'm sorry, but I don't want to listen. You see, the mirrors are coming tomorrow, and already I'm too excited for chit-chat. There are minority interest groups, and they have been in touch. It seems one is not always alone. I boil with newfound desire. Pity those who flew too close to the sun and burned up. But not I; the sun beckons. I am going as far back as it is possible to go. My joy will be in rediscovering how blissful it felt. Remembering.

I have earplugs and a dark hood. And when I get back home I will float, immense, my displacement immense, a pink iceberg, rudely tropical.

From the Chinese of Ssü K'ung T'u

David Purves

The Taoist poet, Ssü K'ung T'u, (834-908) wrote in the later part of the T'ang Dynasty, the Golden Age of Chinese poetry. This was distinguished by the wonderful poetry of Li Po, (702-762), Tu Fu (712-770) and Po Chü-I (772-846). Ssü K'ung T'u belongs here. This was an age of professional poets whom emperors delighted to honour. No lengthy Iliad or Odyssey is to be found in the long tradition of Chinese poetry extending for nearly three millennia, and a favourite feature of later verse are poems which stop short while the sense is projected. The tendency to prune words to a minimum to focus attention on a single experience, heralds the development of the *haiku* format in Japan in the 17th century, against the background of popularity in Japan of Zen Buddhism. This was a product of the merging of a form of Buddhism introduced into China around 500 AD, and Taoism, the entrenched philosophy of Lao Tzu for poets for around a thousand years. The punitive and sacrificial elements associated with the teaching of the Semitic religions have no place in this kind of thinking. The artist is forever striving to capture a moment of awareness from eternity. Nowhere do we encounter the commercial notion of rewards for good conduct at the hands of men or angels.

Earlier Buddhist philosophy, derived from Yogic thought a thousand years earlier, is sometimes criticised as a fatalistic, pessimistic death cult in which, after birth, there is nothing but sorrow; for who can escape death? There are conspicuous aberrations associated with this kind of thinking, such as belief in magic and indifference to physical well-being. All things are *maya* and an illusion. Death may then be seen as a welcome escape from an unreal, worthless illusionary life, for example, from the Chinese of Tendo-Nyojo (1163-1228) we have 'Lest Lowp'.

Lest Lowp

Eftir saxtie-sax year
getherin sins,
Ah lowp inti hell—
abuin Lyfe an Daith

But Ssü K'ung T'u is essentially a positive Taoist poet, for whom reality emerges from the unreal: Spring renews and love and beauty triumph over entropy, death and decay. Little is known about his life except that he retired early from imperial office to lead the contemplative life. The senses are a means of escape from what he perceived as the prison of personality, into boundless freedom. Once the soul is liberated there is no need for aimless wandering. The universe becomes our home and the soul becomes one with it. In entering into harmony with the whole cosmos, Ssü K'ung T'u returns, evidently, to aspects of earlier Yogic thought.

The Tao

Ayont the rax o fashious thocht,
lat us win in til the hert o awthing
an thare haud fest foraye,
fed frae an endless rowth!

The Color o Lyfe

Wad that we micht haud on a wee
til the maikless wattirgaw o the warld,
the unco blue o the bounless sea,
the maivis' sang frae greener Springs langsyne,
the snaw-whyte skinkil in the breingin linn.
Thay sant awa an dwyne foraye throu lyfe,
or even the glisk o maimorie is gaen;
tint oot o sicht at the end for us aw,
binna for a whyle, the infant bairn.

Ma Veision

A drap o wyne brings back the Spring,
doun on the theik an auntrin shour,
a gentil scholar lowdent in the bouer.
Whyte clouds reinge athort the lift abuin.
Syne beildit in the birkenshaw, Ah see
a faemin torrent breinge til the mere.
Aroun ma dremes the deid leifs faw;
lown wi the sterred chrysanthemums,
Ah watch the saison's glories cum an gae,
an read the buiks that never pall.

Quaeit Seil

It bydes in the deep seilence,
unkent on ben an plain
lippert bi tydeless harmonie,
it toves wi the lanesum crane.

As the spring tyme saur whas flauchter
the silken skirts haes blawn,
as the wund-drawn note o the bamboo fluit
whas chairm we wad mak oor awn, –

Chaunce-haird, it kyths ti yield;
socht, an it wyles us ben;
aye-showdin in maik an fantasie,
it jouks us, an is gaen.

Motion

Frae the cawin wattir-wheel
til the yird's gret axis birlin aye
anaith the ever-restless lift abuin,
Ah mell wi awthing inti nocht
ayont the bounds o thocht an dreme,
rinkin the universe wi outlin spheres
whas orbits lests a thousan years
ti win the kie that fits ma theme.

Set Free

Ah im browdent in flouers athout end.
Ah'm an atom at random in space.
The warld is the steid whaur Ah dreme.
Ma saul's in etherial naeplace.

The taps o the swaws Ah touer ower,
mang the wunds o the warld spreidin wyde.
Ah im aw ane wi leimitless pouer,
the haill universe reinged at ma syde.

The above renderings of poems by Ssü K'ung T'u in Scots appear to have a frisson and emotional quality which was not always evident in the English versions from which they were derived. These were translations with an Edwardian flavour by L. Cranmer-Byng, in 'A Lute of Jade', John Murray, London 1909. In general, English translations from a hieroglyphic language like Chinese are recreations which vary widely, and reflect the poetic fashion of the age they were made.

So a whole range of poems in any European phonic language could be created by translating any ancient Chinese poem written in a hieroglyphic script, depending on what was poetically fashionable at the time the translator lived. A translator living in the Kailyard era might confer a post-Burnsian flavour for example, although it might be difficult to render poems by ancient Chinese masters into standard Habbie.

The 170 Chinese poems rendered in English by Arthur Waley (1918) were criticised for not belonging to the English neoclassical tradition with its preoccupation with abstractions and conventional allusions to Greek mythology. The later publication of numerous collections of renderings in English of ancient Chinese poems on both sides of the Atlantic has helped in freeing poetry in English from the shackles of regimented rhyming and metering, and the necessity of making classical allusions to forgotten deities. Contact with Chinese poetry through the medium of English could not, unfortunately, restore the severed connection between English poetry and its social roots in any living community.

Todd Swift

The Lake

All day I would gather deadfall
by his side, fearful and admiring,
watching. He broke off what
he could take, lifted from the leaves.

Now it rises, burnt back to first things:
ash white as a snowy owl.
I rise from dreaming, my father prowls,
throwing his wild beam

to the woods, his shadow a bear's,
dwelling beyond where we'd sleep, in fear.
Nature and madness came together here.
He was worried: thought things no one

else understood: that they would come for us.
The flashed light would sweep across my face
at midnight or at three, lifting me from sleep
and, ordered into the dew or the long webs

I'd wander with him down the lane, silent
as Indian-hunters, each of us with a knife;
a disordered sense of violence in the place
that, during the day, reminded me of peace;

he'd row out, or sleep, or gather in the wood
again, for one more night of burning, fending
off the violent men he said would visit.
I have been in this water; eaten here; slept;

awoken; had wrong visions, and been raised
to break the delicate bond that holds together
the world as it is woven by what happens,
from what never was, except in *imagination*:

that word, that meant a different thing to those
who only drew the veil of things closer
to their faces, not tore it apart, like paper to
kindle another blaze – such repose ruined in

darkness spread: a forest in my father's mind.
I saw one arm of lightning break the afternoon
in half, with the ease of an oar lifting light
across water, its shadow doubling emotion.

Tokyo Elevator Girl

Ginza elevator girl, your sliding white gloves
operating doors in Wako *depot*
offer a flowing constraint, trained
to describe floors in gestures shy yet free:

the gifted caress you impress upon
monotony makes any floating creator envy
your miniaturized way: a slim balance,
uniformed perfection, a glide in control's

direction, art's stays. I'd rise with your
levels for hours, to honour this quiet
mastery, or descend to the ground
where the antique clocks are displayed, even

though unable to say a word you'd get.
Your command of this lifting cubicle
with its set-piece play, classically ruled
to unfold in one time and place excites me.

At The Window

As the water will take you into the premonition of itself,
the day is an immersion. As some animals rise up at the storm

when it changes the windows, so do some lovers say
they can apprehend the approaching death of an owned world

as if it was a pressure in the air that turns an imagination against
the partner of our living, our impression of an otherness.

She will one day lie and never rise again, the moment between
the instant when the sheet-lightning makes the sky flat

as a god pressing into the spaces between water and ice.
So, she shivers in thought at becoming what isn't there anymore.

The Wedding Photographer

I take pictures that build the album,
the looking backwards

to developing beauty:
their standing, happy, just married

after light has changed them.
Into what? Themselves, younger.

It is a private, lonely thing to do,
gathering new pictures of delight.

I lie to recollect their love at night,
no longer the smiling man

who made the families bunch
and grin in lines, angled on stairs,

my dressed self tilted on the hood
of the Jaguar in which they'll ride

The Angel Amateur Boxing Club

The ring's set smack at the heart
of the local club, children
swinging for the red corner or the blue,
to test their mettle against the true measure

of things, the canvas floor.
Boys raise an arm in the final heroic pose,
lifted there by the short man in the bow tie
and the immaculate white shirt.

Mikey is fourteen, a novice junior.
His sisters yell at him in the dirty blue room
as he pounds the face of the smaller one
unable to hold up a glove.

Nobody steps in to hold them apart.
When the weak side throws in the towel
the sigh and whooping of the crowd
is like a kind of violence, a kind of love.

Winter Work In April

I become winter and winter's man
to serve winter in its slow work;
my beard grows like the long span
of some white bird's wing. A stork
is a bird, just as winter is a season.

Having put on winter and winter's cloak
I stalk the white halls, a full blazon
of snow aloft in my long hand
like a new torch. I fold out to expand,
as winter's clock ticks on and on.

Brian Lamont

Famous Last Words

We now come to the award for *Most Popular Phrase or Saying Uttered Before Death.*

Competition in this category is always extremely fierce, and the quality and abundance of terminal epigrams sadly, and perhaps controversially, requires an élite short-list that is absent of many endearing favourites, such as the prophetic 'I'll see you at the top', the melodious 'You're shite and you know you are, you're shite and you know you are', and the uncompromising 'I'm only doing forty!' Each, I am sure you will agree, is an exemplary accompaniment to impending demise and all are worthy of the title.

Nevertheless, after extensive research and meticulous editorial consideration, the nominations are:

'Right, you and me outside – now!'

'Do you know, it's years since I've been on one of these things.'

'I'm just going to pop back for a minute and see if I switched off the gas.'

'Ten, nine, eight ... se-ven ... si ...'

'Well, it doesn't look very safe to me!'

'Sorry to trouble you, but could I borrow your electric hedge trimmer?'

'Honestly, I'm fine.'

'This is fucking great!'

'Oops!'

But the immortal winner is ...

'Don't worry, I know exactly what I'm doing.'

Big Stan

Stanley Henry Johnson was big. He had big broad shoulders, big strong arms, a big red nose and a great big belly. As a matter of fact, everything about Stanley Henry Johnson was big. Stanley Henry Johnson was so big that nobody ever called Stanley Henry Johnson Stanley Henry Johnson. By affectionately abbreviating his name and devising a unique frame of reference to describe his inordinate bulk, everyone who knew Stanley Henry Johnson just called him Big Stan.

'Alright "Big Stan",' people would ask when they passed him in the street. Or, 'Have you seen "Big Stan" lately?' they might ask each other if he hadn't been seen around for a while.

Mrs Williams, Big Stan's next-door neighbour, always called Big Stan 'Big Stan'. She called him 'Big Stan' when she came round the other night and banged on his front door.

'"Big Stan",' she shouted through the letterbox. '"Big Stan", do you think you could turn the music down a bit, it's four o'clock in the morning?'

She could see his big boots lying in the hallway and his big overcoat beside, but there was no sign of Big Stan.

The 'Tale' o Tam McInness

A warrior in days o auld,
Renowned fir being brave an bold.
Yet only I have lived tae say
Whit cut him doon yon fatal day.

He'd trashed his way doon through the glen,
The deed lay stroon aboot him, then,
At last, at the end o his tether,
Sat doon astride a sprig o heather.

Oh! The tears o pain streamed doon his cheeks,
For wishing noo he'd worn his breeks.
That sharp surprise and lack o warning
Had ruined Tam's entire morning.

First Impressions, *a humorous collection of stylised writing by Brian Lamont, was published in 2005. Penbury Press, PO Box 28268, Edinburgh, EH9 1ZL. Email: penburypress@yahoo.co.uk Web-site: http//:penburypress.blogspot.com*

Editorial Note: *Mr Lamont's Famous Last Words was irresistible due to its resonances with the Chapman 'reject letter', which disappointed aspiring contributors to the magazine will immediately recognise!*

Frances Campbell

Workers On A Station Platform

See that cunt there?
Whit cunt?
That wan ah'm pointin at.
Whit aboot 'im?
'S a pure cunt, that.
Izz 'at right?
Aye, 'cause nae cunt, hear me, nae cunt
caas me whit that cunt caaed me,
'cept ma mither, unnerstand?
Whit d'he caa ye?

Son.

Cunnilingus

Frances Campbell

"Ye cannnae get in unless ye know the password? Whit's the password?"

"Fish 'n chips."

"Alright, on you go!"

Do you mind of that? When you were a kid and a password could be bread 'n jam? See if someone had told me then that by the time I hit forty there'd be more passwords about than during the entire Cold War I'd have told them to boil their heads. And now it's all this Chip n' Pin. Life was simpler when I was a boy. Then it was cops 'n robbers. Now I'm sitting here in the nick for real. And all because I gave my password away.

Whit did you want to do that for? I hear you asking. I know ... that's whit they're all askin – as if I was a vestal virgin and it was the key to my chastity belt.

But naw, it was the password to my computer at work. My other work. At Ticket World in the town. They sell tickets for concerts and shows all over the country. Price of them. Unbelievable, the amount of money changes hands. And of course our job is to take folks' credit card details over the phone. Well, their details were safe wi me. Not that I'm dead honest or nothing. I'd rob a bank tomorrow if I thought I could get away wi it. But no wi my luck. Here's me done sweet F A and still behind bars. Honest Joe. Naw, I've never considered fraud. Least no for more 'n a second or two. And maybe that's how it never occurred to me a colleague would want to do me over.

Jennifer, that was her name, the girl ... woman, whatever you want to call her. I know what I want to call her. Ay, she took my password. Alright – so I offered it first. I was between a rock and a hard place, see. Two jobs. One at an insurance company from nine till five. Then taking calls at Ticket World four evenings a week. Trouble was the Ticket World job started at quarter past five. Which gave me exactly fifteen minutes to make the half hour trip across town. Russell, the manager, had pulled me into his office for lateness already.

"Look I'm sorry about your circumstances. About your wife, I mean. But this is a business not a charity and you freely contracted to turn up regularly for work at five fifteen. If you can't keep to the agreed times I'm going to have to let you go."

I could feel my neck grow hot listening to his spiel. I have to wear a shirt for the insurance job. And there's no time to freshen up between jobs given that I'm running late every day. "Freely contracted!" I said. "How freely contracted can a man stretched over a barrel be?' I let him have it. "My wife suffers from M.S. She canny work. Man, I need this job.

We've four weans and it takes two salaries just getting by."

"Like I said, Joe, this is not a charity. I'm concerned with operational matters and from where I'm standing, you need to raise your game."

Me! And him hanging over me wi breath reekin' of onions too! I tell you, he has only my Claire to thank for the fact that I didn't rearrange his features right then. She keeps me in order. Smart lady. She used to do the books for a firm down the town. Good money. I was drivin tankers then. Trundling across the Pennines, steering hundreds of gallons of fuel across black ice.

Well, what wi my Claire needing a hand, I gave up the road so I could be home at night. And nights is about the only time I get home these days. I'm at Ticket World till 11 pm. Then back at Crapitol Insurance first thing in the morning. Then scoot across town with my bum on fire, cutting up everyone else on the road and still getting in well past starting time.

It was after the blow-out with Russell I hit on the idea of giving Jennifer my password.

"See, if you log me onto my computer after you've logged onto your own they'll never guess I'm not here yet. I'll just saunter in later with my shirt sleeves rolled up as if I've been to the toilet or something."

Jennifer raised an eyebrow and looked at me with her mouth all pursed. "I'm not sure. What if one of the managers catches on?"

"Just act daft. Plead ignorance. Come on, Jen. If I lose this job, it'll be Claire and the kids who'll feel it not me. Have you any idea how much weans cost? I've four from six to sixteen and there's not a day goes by without one of 'em needing something new."

She kind of lowered her head and looked around then whispered: "Alright, what's your password then?"

I went hot from the collar upwards for a change. It just proves how much I hadnae thought it through. Because if I had, I would've changed my password before I spoke to Jennifer.

She tutted. "Look, if you don't want to give me it ..."

"No it's just ..."

"What?"

"Cunnilingus."

"Excuse me?"

"You heard." I shuffled about wi my feet.

"Is this your way of getting a perverted thrill at my expense?"

"No, honest. I never thought I'd need to reveal it. My password at my other work is..."

"No, stop. I can guess."

"Sorry, just my way of bringing a touch of humanity into the loveless world of machines."

"Leave it, will you? So what happens if you drop dead and don't turn up one day?"

"Like my old Grandad used to say, Where there's necrophilia, there's hope." She went stiff as a corpse at that and I knew I'd gone too far. My Claire enjoys a bit of repartee but see young women now. Any-ways, I back-pedalled on the spot. "Sorry Jen, look – let me make this worth your while. What about cheap holiday insurance, is that any use to you?"

"Could be."

"Right, I'll fix you up wi vouchers from my other work."

"*Muchas gracias*. Can you get them for my boyfriend too? He works in a bank but free's better than staff discount any day."

"Spain is it? *Nul problemo*. And, like I said, anyone asks you about the password, just play dumb."

"I'm not sure I know how." She tossed her head of greasy blond hair. But so what if she'd no time to stay home and shampoo it. Wisnae my type anyway.

For the first week everything went fine then one night she hissed at me between calls. "I'm not prepared to use that password any more. It makes me squirm."

Sensitive lady. Someone as sensitive as that – makes you think they're above board somehow.

"Sure, Jennifer." I tilted back in my seat, fanning my face with a mouse mat. "Is there another word you'd like to suggest?" I gave her my most impish, little boy smile.

"What about Adventuress?"

My turn to raise an eyebrow now.

"Well," she said. "It is a bit chancy, this sort of scam."

I didn't think of it as a scam myself. Pure survival, that's all it was. I was still shooting across town with my bum on fire. It's not as if I was going to be putting my feet up while she was typing 'Adventuress' into a dialog box. What sort of adventure was she on about anyway?

So all is calm for a few weeks then one day I'm doing the old quick-slow over the threshold as usual and there's Russell standing by his office saying: "Joe, would you step in here?"

I looked round the work stations for Jennifer but her desk was empty. Damn, I should have given her my mobile number so she could text me if she was taking a sickie. Russell smelled of aftershave. He starts his shift at three. I had a day's sweat stiff on my shirt already.

"Look Joe, since we last spoke your time-keeping has improved remarkably. Of course, there are other performance issues. Your tone, for instance. You often sound tired, bored even. The voice monitor is picking it up. Try to remember that when callers ring for concert tickets they're buying into a good experience all down the line. A little enthusiasm wouldn't go amiss."

"Yeah," I shrugged. What can you say? I just let him know I'd heard him, that's all.

"But getting back to the time-keeping issue. Why the slip up?" He looked at his watch. "I make it five fifty now."

"Sorry, I was held up. Is Jennifer not in today?"

"No. Didn't she tell you? She's left."

"Never said a dicky bird. Where's she gone?"

"South America. One of those two year adventure trips. She and her boyfriend have been planning it for a while, working all hours to get up the funds."

"Ay," I said. "That's the sort of thing folk usually work all hours for."

He just looked through me. Wouldn't rise to the challenge. Might as well replace him wi a machine as well.

So. The Adventuress had drifted off, leaving me up shit creek without a paddle. I drummed my fingers on my desk then approached a couple of other women to see if they could help me out. By the way their mouths dropped open you'd have thought I was asking for a rummage in their knicker drawers.

Three nights later Russell called me into his office again. A big uniformed polis was standing beside him and my first thought was Claire and the kids.

"What's up? My wife ...?" I stuck in the doorway, heart racing while the rest of me was nailed to the carpet tiles.

Russell said: "Would you please come in and shut the door? The police would like to ask you some questions."

My mind was all over the shop. When the police stop you on the road, you generally have an idea what you've done. Broken tail lights, speeding, unstable load.

"Inspector Dunn here is from the fraud squad," said Russell. For the first time I noticed the woman in a designer suit sitting at his desk. She closed the lid of her laptop and waved towards a seat for me.

"For some time callers buying tickets from this centre have had their credit card details used fraudulently. Most of the details have been used to transfer sums of money into a bank account which is now closed. We're talking about at least £30,000 pounds. Have you anything to say?"

"Thirty thousand pounds! Do you think I'd be standing here in my What Every's V-neck if I had thirty thousand stashed away!"

Inspector Dunn looked me up and down like a woman who knew mass market gear was the downside of her job. Zero for people skills. "Several victims made only one credit card transaction in the last month and this has enabled us to trace the fraud directly to this centre and one particular agent. You."

It's not often I am rendered speechless. But right then my tongue floundered. The pure shock of it.

"Is there anything you'd like to add?"

I just looked at them as I struggled to find my voice. It had slipped away, way down to a big black hole inside me somewhere. I found it just as the big polis was leading me out through the phone hall.

"It wisnae me!" I cried. "It wisnae me!"

All the folk at their computers were staring at me like when you're watching one of those Roman gladiator movies and the Emperor gives the thumb down. That's what it felt like. Thumbs down. When the real crook could have been any one of them.

But, of course, I put two and two together while I was cooling off in the cell. Jennifer. She could type in my password, take calls and the records would make it look like me. That from the woman who was snooty about a little foreplay. She'd done me over well and good. I jumped off my bench and shook the bars. "It's a set up! Tell the inspector. That wee minger was conning me!"

They got me back up to the interview room then. I was talking nineteen to the dozen. "See if I get the jail, my kids will need to go into care. Claire's not able for the younger ones. Have you thought of that? So where's my motivation? If I had that Jennifer in front of me now. She'd be dead meat, I'm telling you."

The inspector glanced up from her screen. "I've been checking your password history. Frankly, it reads like a toilet door. And we only have your word for this Jennifer story. The fact is, you can't prove you weren't logged on, taking credit card details at the exact times given. "

She's not very bright, Inspector Dunn. Needs to polish up the basics, I'd say.

"Ay, I can prove I wisnae there."

She waits and I let her. Draw out the tension. I look round the room, out the wee window then into her eyes. "Check my computer at Crapitol Insurance. You'll see I was logged on there every night till five. And if you can cut across town in less than half an hour you should be locked up yourself." I could tell by the way her face crumpled that she was beat. This was now a case for Interpol.

"I'll just make a few calls to verify your story," she said. "If you'd like to take a seat in the corridor. There's no need to return to your cell."

"An apology wouldn't be out of line."

She glared like a cat with its tail trod on so I just left in case she locked me up again.

Ay, who ever thought I'd need an alibi? Or that I'd have a computer to thank for getting me out of this mess? But no more Mr Nice Guy. That Jennifer had better stay in South America a very long time – and if she claims insurance she'll be sorry, as well. I'm gonna lose my job through her. Damn near lost my freedom too. But leastways I could use a break. And I've another wee project on the boil. There's a poster up on the wall in front of me in this corridor. Criminal Injuries Compensation Board. That could be worth a bob or two. I think I've been a victim here.

Tessa Ransford

Edinburgh, April Evening

Herring gull on a chimney pot
above and around crosses, crowns,
corbelling, even a sphinx;
clock strikes from St Giles
in a sky of delicate clouds
as shadows revolve
on dome, copula, stone
of Edinburgh's Old Town.

Aeroplane silvers across
above and around gull-nested crags
and the spikey new parliament
(infested it seems by doves).
A crude red lion with blue claws
on the Queen's Gallery
not rampant except for commerce -
has no roar for the politicians.

By Canongate Kirk the poet is walking
in sculpture, Robert Fergusson,
before his fall and desolate death.
He clutches his youthful poems which
berate the wily lawyers and praise
'the braid cloth' of plain speaking in Scots.
Above him cherry trees bow, and bless
that inner life of literature, unmanageable and alive.

Portrait of Girl at the Piano

I open the door
to music
rosewood from the piano
and a young girl playing
bare-thighed in her nightshirt
toes at the pedal
her hair tied back
and slanting neck inclined towards
the music she brings from
her expertise, her
casual confidence, her
imminent maturity.

Women's Secret Language in China

Secret language
for women, for only
women, mother to
daughter over and under

How we enjoy and how
we adapt, what children need,
when to hold on and
when to let go, what the body
knows, where we are strong,
why we live long

Renewable wisdom: endure,
listen, hear, wait, watch,
welcome, encourage, restore

Spindly signs like needle marks:
share, safekeep,
embrace, praise

Fury, mercy, laughter,
laughter, will soon,
all die but
our language will
surpass itself.

In My Bones

Bones in dust, dust from bones
of pre-ice-age humans;
tests discover how they fed:
mammoth, reindeer, bear, fox
salmon, seal, wild cats.

What I eat in my bones:
chocolate, pasta, tinned tomato
and a lifetime of potato
fish, butter, bread and rice
tea, marmite, orange juice.

Drill my bones, shake the dust
nothing shows how I am fed
by poetry, music, children, friends
paintings, letters, photographs
undetectable to those
who dig my bones millennia hence?

Shona Dougall illustration to 'Blue Gate'

Blue Gate

after Winifred Nicholson's painting 'Gate to the Isles'

Blue gate alone on the hill
no attachment to fence or wall
no pathway before, behind
open to nothing and all.

Faded gate on the machair
broken, blistered your paint;
the homestead once you guarded
a heap of rubbled neglect.

Once you led to the grazing,
to garden or lazybed;
the sound of a click on the latch
brought neighbour, welcomed, fed.

Blue gate where do you open
out of and into the blue –
we pass with a wistful smile
and let our wishes through.

The Dreams I Have

The dreams I have are all of the dead
my mother and father who never fail
to encompass me wherever I'm led

The husband who loved my poems and read
them with often a believing smile
comforts my dreams although now dead

The kindly woman from Wazirabad
who helped me when the children were small
is often around wherever I'm led

Long-ago friends and Vera who fed
my mind and heart with talk and tale
appear in my dreams despite being dead

It seems as if they are free and glad
to emerge as if in answer to call
and encompass me wherever I'm led.

A Sign for Our Time

Disgorged from a beached whale
Jonah gave warning to Nineveh
and that great city paid heed.

The whale itself came to London
on a suicide mission to save.
It struggled far up the Thames
level with Westminster.

Thousands gawked at the whale
a northern bottle-nosed beauty
and experts tried to save it.

They said it had lost its way
and wasn't too well. But it came to warn
that the planet is ailing and that
it is we who have lost our way.

The Story of Andrew Gilligan

I'll tell you the story of Andrew Gilligan
beware – it may make your blood run chill again:
the sexed-up dossier may make you ill again
that sent our lads to be killed and to kill again
the weapons-inspectors finding nil again
the holes in the desert we dig up and fill again
the contracts for oil and rattling the till again
the public who has to, yes, pay the bill again
for spin and lies, the won'ts and the will again
the beans the media's forbidden to spill again
David Kelly they can't now grill again
Little Jack Straw tumbling downhill again
sipping his bedtime *Horlicks* swill again
Campbell and his marching on-off drill again
Blair and Bush cocks of the world's dunghill again
Gordon Brown sitting quiet and still again
Kofi Annan goes through the mill again
Robin Hood Cook with his bitter pill again
Greg Dyke waving defiant farewell again
Butler says *they all meant well* again
It looks as if no heads will roll again
we could join 'old Europe' and bring back the guillotine:
it's enough to make your blood run chill again
the too true story of Andrew Gilligan.

Stewart Conn's 'Realm of Possibility'

Colin Nicholson

When Edinburgh City Council appointed Stewart Conn as Makar in 2002, it was an interesting choice not least because although Conn has lived in the capital for the past thirty years, he is not native to the city and that fact did not escape him. Yet by the time he resigned from running the BBC's Scottish Radio Drama Department ten years earlier he had already made a substantial contribution to our cultural life through the drama he has directed over the years and the poets he broadcast. In his own right he has an impressive number of stage and radio plays to his name; as well as a body of poetry that traces evolving perspectives on subjectivity and place. He was, at any rate, a well-qualified candidate for Edinburgh's first modern Makar: his third collection, *An Ear to the Ground* (1972) was a Poetry Book Society Choice, and in 2000 Conn's *Stolen Light: Selected Poems* (1999, hereafter *SP*) was short-listed for the Saltire Book of the Year award. But the Makar invitation was a complete surprise to him:

[SC] *It came absolutely out of the blue. When Paul Scott [of the Saltire Society] telephoned I thought at first that he was sounding me on the idea of an Edinburgh Laureateship, and I assumed that he was either lobbying for somebody or wondering if I would back a particular candidate. Then he announced that I had been chosen, and would I meet with himself and the Director of Culture and Leisure because the appointment was to be made under the City Council's umbrella.*

Conn accepted there and then, but he did have qualms about it.

[SC] *Firstly, having been born in Glasgow and growing up in Ayrshire, becoming the Edinburgh Makar was the last thing in the world I could have expected. Then, secondly, Makar is medieval Scots for poet, and though its resonant association excited me, the fact is I don't write in Scots. But I can only write the way that I do and if having done that I was approached for the post, then that was their decision. It made me realise nevertheless how times have changed in Edinburgh since, say, the time of Sydney Goodsir Smith and Robert Garioch when I suspect there would have been a* furore *if it had not been a Scots-writing poet.*

But he was comfortable with the open-ended approach to his duties:

[SC] *There was no brief to write civic verse, which I was very relieved about, but it was assumed that I would write poems relating to Edinburgh, and I myself obviously felt under an obligation to respond to this. There would also be a number of readings and workshops and talks to give: and the emphasis would by my choice be on Edinburgh poetry rather than my own poetry.*

So Conn's term of office involved an interesting learning curve:

[SC] *I had to work on Fergusson, and one of the glories to me of my Makardom has been a rediscovery, a re-attuning of my regard for Fergusson and his work, and the fact that during my tenure I was asked to write a poem for the unveiling of David Annand's sprightly statue of Fergusson in the Canongate.*

For reasons that become interesting in relation to a Scottish social narrative of regional identification and displacement, and in spite of a long-term creative residence in Edinburgh, when Conn took up his laureateship he still harboured doubts about his place in the city:

[SC] *There was still an element missing. 'A sense of belonging' is a phrase in one of my early poems and it was picked up as the title of an anthology of mainly West of Scotland writing. I felt I didn't belong in Edinburgh, although I knew my mother had been born and gone to university here.*

This was not the first time a sense of belonging had caused him anxiety. In one of his essays about people and places in his life Conn recalls how, years after he left to live and work in Glasgow, he went back to Kilmarnock for a writer's workshop, still confident that "through my own accent and peppering of Scots, I had retained at least a residual trace of my Ayrshire upbringing". In the event Conn was "forcefully told: 'You're no frae Killie. You're bliddy English!', so mim-mou'd had I evidently become: one penalty perhaps, of supping ower-lang with the BBC" (Stewart Conn, *Distances: A Personal Evocation of People and Places p 20,* hereafter *D*). But this was small beer compared with what he encountered as director of Scottish radio drama. The Drama Department had been moved from Glasgow to Edinburgh in 1976, Conn with it, and there has never been much love lost between the two cities, with a history of social, economic and cultural competitiveness in which rival accents become a marker of class-conscious differentiation as well as a source for much satire and stand-up comedy. And Conn is openly aware about how he has remained, [SC] *"some would say imprisoned, within the cage of my middle classness and my middle class diction"*. Not surprisingly he had felt his cage being directly rattled [SC] *"at the time when Tom Leonard was writing in reaction very much to what was happening in Edinburgh and to BBC English particularly, which he satirises beautifully in one of his poems"*.

Glasgow's demotic sound world animates the work of various writers, and the continuing viability of regionally distinctive speech remains a lively political issue. Tom Leonard's cultural take on the Glasgow he was born into is often hilarious, while his phonetic transcription of working class vernacular is a finely honed instrument. So the structure of feeling that Leonard communicates gives point to Conn's anxiety, who may have had in mind the poem spoken by a BBC Six o'Clock newsreader in Leonard's orchestrated series of 'Unrelated Incidents':

if
a toktaboot
thi trooth

lik wanna yoo
scruff yi
widny thingk
it wuz troo.

(Tom Leonard, *Intimate Voices*)

While Conn learned to arm himself with what he called "elements of the Glaswegian suspiciousness of the snobbery, supposed snobbery, the class and English accents in Edinburgh", his creative output, and his drama department's, continued unabated, perhaps because Conn's sense of who he was had considerable resources of its own to call on; not least a humane and civilised Presbyterian upbringing in a secure and sustaining family. Douglas Dunn's entry for Conn in the *Oxford Companion to Twentieth Century Poetry in English* mentions his "unmodish awareness of [life's] decencies and delights", in which "subdued rhythms ... and a plain vocabulary are characteristic of his unassertive but attractively honest voice" (p 98). This may understate the striking effects Conn can achieve, but it catches the crafted restraint that typifies his verse.

Conn was a son of the manse, his father a Church of Scotland minister who was enlightened in many of his attitudes and who "never tried to force me to join Church. I never did" (*D* 16). The poetry articulates secular values, and both the relationship and the distance between Conn and his father's customary field of reference are effectively registered when a recent poem justifies a realm of possibility by foregrounding its own constructions over authorised versions. 'In the Garden' discloses interactive memory and perception when sunlight on "a golden choisya", an orange blossom known as Sundance, prompts thoughts of the fabled bush which burned undamaged while an Old Testament godhead spoke from it directly to Moses. The speaker remembers seeing this image of fiery deliverance, which has been widely adopted as a Scottish Presbyterian icon and badge of self-identification, on hymnals in his father's church. It is germane to Conn's existential perspectives that the poem's "impression/ of a nimbus" derives instead from sunshine on a garden plant, and so 'comes untrammelled/ by such baggage". 'In the Garden' extends the thought world and sifts the values of a paternal ambience it varies into humanist invention when its speaker thinks of a nearby butterfly "as more likely to be Li Po/ dreaming, than the alter ego/ of a Presbyterian divine/ sermonising on sin" (Stewart Conn, *Ghosts at Cockcrow*, p12), thereby implicating another belief system in its witty alternatives, so that the poem can deliver free-thinking metaphor in place of biblical prescription.

St Marnock's Parish Church is near Kilmarnock town centre and as Minister, Conn's father was representatively middle class in a largely working class and economically depressed area that was coping with hard times in the post-war 1940s. In Kilmarnock, Conn remembers, "the dominant atmosphere was one of cosy congregationalism" (*D* 14), but because his father's relations worked a nearby farmstead, young Conn was able to spend his Saturdays and school holidays on the family holding at Harelaw in Craigie parish, three miles south of Ayr. Five years old when the family left Glasgow Hillhead for Kilmarnock, he was already moving within and across some of Scotland's different social borders and class divides, and that movement would subsequently animate his memorable series of Ayrshire poems. He could not have known at the time that he was witnessing the end of an era. The larger-than-life characters he met at Harelaw farm have gone the way of all flesh, joining the already semi-legendary and long-departed relatives he learned about from stories he heard there. The farm itself has vanished, much of it levelled to make way for urban housing schemes. Conn went back in later years and noted how the surviving "farmlands [which] had come to be identified with my youth" were now "remote and irretrievable". In that identification personal memories generate cultural resonance from a relentless economic decline in the area from the 1970s onwards, and Conn comments on this, too. So when he writes "If I felt I belonged anywhere it was on those tilled and tilted acres; in the knowes and their lime-pits where a horse and cart were said to have plunged and disappeared; on those pastures and quarry-slopes" (*D* 19, 23), we hear his conditional mood; and 'disappeared' echoes in the mind.

The Harelaw poems reconstruct a sense of compromised belonging out of the times and places of schoolboy sights and sounds by exploring relationship between responses at the time of writing and remembered thoughts and feelings from a changed world. Fleeting impressions become a matter of language and memory virtually in the moment they signify, and Conn is good at finding forms of definition that register impermanence as they vivify incident. The title poem of his first collection, *Thunder in the Air* (1967), focuses on a boy's secret possession of fields and foliage where there is "No need for disguises/ And no need to reveal/ The beauty of this place". But a need to reveal and connect remembered places motivates the writing, and 'Harelaw' from his second book *Stoats in the Sunlight* (1968), sees disinheritance as radical disturbance in the ecological rhythms of a once locally-sustaining environment. Its first three stanzas bear witness to what is no longer there before the speaker reconstructs for his younger self a sense of possession that had seemed secure, and a still-unquestioned imaginative ownership of his family's farm: "mine/ To siege and plunder; here I caged/ Rare beasts or swayed royally on the agèd/ Backs of horses – here hacked my secret sign,/ Strode, wallowed, ferreted, rampaged". But material "acres crumple", the remembering speaker continues, "and the farm's new image/ Spreads over the old". Enough of the farm's old image survives in the final stanza to express the observer's discordant mood:

As I face
Its change, a truck tips litter; hens assess
Bright tins, then peck and squawk their rage.
The truck spurts flame and I have no redress. (*SP*, 23)

Confronting irretrievable alteration, the poems exploit a west of Scotland farmland setting in the hope of retaining "an enduring sense of possession, albeit through dispossession" (*D* 23), partly by breathing life into memories associated with an awesome great-uncle who had a powerful impact on a growing boy. That great-uncle, Todd Cochrane, managed to be both caring and expert with horses (and a successful horse-dealer until demand failed), and a Presbyterian sectary – "His talk all of Jacob, of Moses/ And Aaron, of Daniel in the lions' den" (*SP* 20) – who sacked a landgirl for whistling on a Sunday. It seems an irony of fate that Todd was also a versifier, from whom young Conn first heard native west of Scotland speech in rhyme. When his great-uncle recited verse (interminably, as Conn remembers) and asked "Well, who do you think wrote that?" the boy soon learned what was "a ritual everyone in the family underwent, at one time or another", by giving the required response. "Robbie Burns, Uncle?" "Not a bit of it. It was masel." (*D* 20).

Because his great-uncle's own "fire and brimstone verses were in the tongue he customarily spoke", the sound left a lasting impression: it was through Ayrshire farming relations from a bygone way of life that Conn probably came as close to the sound-world Burns moved through and recorded as anyone is likely to get. Meanwhile, the speech and cadence he heard on Craigie Hill were a far cry and a world away from the socially acceptable modes that were simultaneously promoted in the classroom:

> At Kilmarnock Academy in my day Scots was tolerated in Burns, but clamped down on otherwise. The poems and songs were approved as art-objects; but to be severed in our minds and tongues from any wider social or cultural context. … No such dichotomy on the farm. There the poems registered on my ear as patterned extension of common speech, not as elocution exercises. (*D* 21)

By writing the past into the present as direct recall, the Harelaw poems transmit once-known community as memory shaped by prior story, and that is where myths are made as Conn is well aware. *Distances* remembers great-uncle Todd as "a cross between the White Knight and an Old Testament prophet" (p 20), and the much-anthologised poem 'Todd', memorialising a man who died "when the mechanised tractor came to pass", turns its subject's biblical phrasing and religious thought world into surreal comedy: "Now I think of him neighing to some saint/ in a simple heaven or, beyond complaint,/ leaning across a fence and munching grass" (*SP* 15). The persistence of memory, and of the need to reconstruct its contexts and feelings, is a marked feature of this early writing, where the processes of personal perception become an exercise in self-definition as well as a convincing mode of delivery. "I can still see him" is the opening phrase in the first of a 'Todd' sequence of six poems, and in the final lines of the last one we read:

I still see him
Come cantering out to the yard, his brown serge
Suit streaming, the horses under him neighing
And neighing. No more than half real. At once
Fabulous and absurd: like Goya, who went painting
At night with candles round the brim of his hat. (*SP* p 23)

Because memory must operate in a remembering present, inevitably transforming the past it shapes into its presenting language, the poem projects its own remembering perception as much as the remembered figure who shades into delusory effect. A once-living character becomes a matter of textual representation as much as of recall, a figure of invention as much as a family relative.

For an adult speaker standing 'On Craigie Hill', the childhood farm that forms a focus for several of these early poems already "seems centuries ago". Where remembered context is already partially visualised "from coloured prints"; and where "Too much has changed, is still changing", it becomes correspondingly "hard to look/ back with any sense of belonging". In this poetics of loss, memory extends into a longer perspective by reaching back to a father's childhood in the same place:

This blustery afternoon on Craigie Hill
I regard remotely the muddy track
My father used to trudge along, to school. (*SP* p. 26)

To the extent that all memory-writing reconstructs possible versions of selfhood, it constitutes a realm of fiction, not least because with the distance of time it is impossible to determine "how much was inserted in the mind's eye by hearsay – or old photographs; these in turn contributing (and applying a time scale) to many of my poems" *(D* 56-7). Identifying a rooted social ancestry was important to Conn, who can legitimately claim that "no matter how mythologised my memories have become, or how fanciful they may have been in the first place", the poems that inscribe them "remain related to real people – a sturdy people who belonged to a specific soil, as it belonged (for a while) to them" (*D* 23).

His success in delivering specific contours of experience for contexts of change and separation helped to establish Conn's early reputation: his attention to the fugitive and fleeting elements in experience remains central to his verse. Historical memory is a necessary element in that recovery. "Where", asks the poem 'Te Maori', "might the spirits of our ancestors reside?" It is "Up to us", the final lines suggest, "to preserve/ our own repositories of intuition" (*SP* 185). The achieved definition of Vermeer's 'Kitchen Maid' (*SP* p 85) gives rise to the suggestion that "We are ourselves/ suspended in space"; and what Douglas Dunn called

Conn's "unnerving sense of the fragility of life" (p 98), is expertly registered by a nervous skater on thin ice in the title poem of Conn's fourth collection, *Under the Ice* (1978), who "watches my shadow on the water below", and is led to wonder "whether the real you/ pirouettes in space,/ or beckons from under the ice/ for me to come through" (*SP* 83). Ghosts both spooky and seemingly real appear as name, figure and shadowy presence early and late. The ghost of completed assonance sounds in Conn's prevalent use of half-rhymes: his need to associate fleeting impressions with the physical durability of stone, architecture and statuary also characterises a body of writing where paintings and artwork that have stood the test of time become a favoured resource.

All of these elements play a part in Conn's latest collection, named from G M Trevelyan's phrase for human transience, *Ghosts at Cockcrow.* The source in Trevelyan is identified in an epigraph that has wider relevance to Conn's characteristic forms of attention:

> Once, on this earth, once, on this familiar spot of ground, walked other men and women, as actual as we are today, thinking their own thoughts, swayed by their own passions, but now all gone, one generation vanishing after another, gone as utterly as we ourselves shall shortly be gone like ghosts at cockcrow. (*Ghosts*, p 51)

While the poems find occasion for appearances, sightings, ways of seeing and "reminders of impermanence" (p 18) in locations from Burgundy to Barcelona, from Ely Cathedral to Washington DC, threads of connection register. A visitor to the Besançon countryside notes: "Remote areas are possessed by the ghosts of those/ who tilled the soil in an age more rural than ours", and is struck by "an absence of song-birds" and no sign of cockerels: "Strange were these/ to become a thing of the past, their raucous cocoricos/ remote and irretrievable as our fugitive desires" (56).

This latest collection also includes the poems Conn produced as Edinburgh's Makar and so brings us back to his laureate duties:

[SC] The wording of the brief was to heighten the profile of poetry in Edinburgh and as I saw it to raise the profile of Edinburgh in poetry – both ways. I was aware of my obligation not just to Edinburgh, which sounds pompous, but to myself. I didn't want to be an Edinburgh spokesman in other words, I didn't want any suggestion of that, and the instinctive way to do it was to write poems recognisably set in Edinburgh; so there's a sequence of poems set in the Royal Mile, which touches on closes and touches on history.

The first poem, 'Realm of Possibility', opens recognisably on an Edinburgh study covered by plasterers' dust-sheets and coated with fine powder, and closes on expectations of further discovery: "In due course I'll note any emergence / from this unseasoned whiteness":

> Or who knows, discover the spoor
> of some elusive creature
> and track it to its lair. (*Ghosts* 11)

As its first incumbent, Conn had an open brief to craft an identity as Edinburgh's Makar. If we turn the tracking in 'Realm of Possibility' to autobiographical account, then what Conn calls his "spider's webs of genealogy in family history", this time on his mother's side, were a help with Edinburgh context. He had already traced one of her distant ancestors back to the Ettrick graveyard where James Hogg is buried, and felt "as though some element within me had been somehow resolved, put at rest, in this little kirkyard nestling amidst the soft contours of the Border hills" (D 67). Of more localised relevance and from a nearer branch, Conn knew that his maternal grandfather, originally from Selkirk, had owned a grocer's shop in Edinburgh, but he didn't discover until just after his appointment that it was located in the Royal Mile (High Street) of Edinburgh's Old Town. 'Heirloom' starts the Royal Mile series by suggesting that this family link to place helped Conn "feel less an interloper,/ than one who has been long away" (*Ghosts*, 35):

[SC] I felt I didn't have to struggle to grasp at something outside myself, but that it was more a question of having the confidence of a conviction that something would come from inside myself. And something did, but for me in the most unexpected way in a single poem-sequence in the new volume, the 'Roull of Corstorphin' sequence.

In Edinburgh's National Library, a few weeks before his term of office ended, Conn read 'Roull of Corstorphin' embellished by John Sampson's period accompaniment on a variety of wind instruments. It was an interesting experiment in performance art, where contemporary representations of historical harmony and invented Renaissance voice entertainingly coincided. The conjunction brought to light how far Conn was grasping at something outside and how much came from within, which becomes a theme in the 'Roull' sequence. From the beginning Conn has made skilled use of genealogy to posit versions of self that relate to specific times and places. Now he was Edinburgh's laureate with a string of publications behind him delivering in speech and print a possible early Renaissance literary ancestor who has left nothing other than his name on the record. I asked Conn to instruct my ignorance:

[SC] If it's a level of ignorance it's one that I totally shared, which is why I started to explore it. There's the reference in Dunbar's 'Lament for the Makars' about death taking 'Roull of Aberdene,/ And gentil Roull of Corstorphin'; and Sibbald's Chronicles of Scottish Poetry *refers to "a poem in the Bannatyne Ms called Rowll's cursing". That led me to Lindsay's* Testament and Complaynt of Our Soverane Lordis Papyngo *(1538), which quotes three stanzas attributed to a Roull, but it doesn't say which one. And if Dunbar wrote his poem in 1508 or whatever and Roull is in it; that means he predeceased Dunbar.*

Who was he? Nothing's known, I knew nothing, where do we start? I started with 'Roull Posited' which wonders, was he a priest, was he teacher, but ends by describing him as 'the capital's earliest recorded poet'. In the second poem I observed him at a court flyting, but took the word 'gentil' over-literally to make him a lyric poet which I have an affinity with, rather than a political or a flyting poet.

As the sequence sets its constructed subject in cultural context, Roull becomes a credible figure of invention, a believable fiction enlivened by the way Conn connects the spaces between the few fleeting mentions the record had left him to work with. Since two Roulls are named there, he makes the cursing one an Aberdeen flyter and imagines them as cousins, corresponding with each other in poems 3 and 4, which retains an Old Scots flavour by including an italicised stanza taken word for word from the Bannatyne manuscript – [SC] "except for 'the dry boak' which I put in at the end to get myself out of it". Then, having directed John Purser's play about the Scottish Renaissance composer Robert Carver, Conn felt comfortable bringing Carver into poem 5, 'Roull on Musik Fyne'.

The possibility of interactive identification took a formative turn when Conn followed up a suggestion John Purser made, by including a piece called 'In Time of Plague'. He had written the poem years earlier when his two sons were boys, but was unable until now to bring it into print [SC] "because I felt it was too direct and I would have felt awkward putting it in a book". Finding a place for personal intimacy in the 'Roull' sequence sealed a bond between writer and subject which brings the story of Conn's self-inventions up to date:

[SC] *I was living Roull, as I've never lived a poem in my life. I've never written anything that length before – I know it's broken up but I still think of it as being one sequence. I'd given something of myself with 'In time of Plague', because I was able to say it as Roull or let Roull say it as me.*

Who is speaking as whom becomes moot in the lyric called 'In Seikness' which introduces a form of utterance closer to one Conn first heard in Scotland's rural west. The design of the sequence makes the voice Roull's, but Stewart Conn is testing relationship by writing effectively in Scots; and 'To his Wife' could credibly belong to either poet. When Roull's ghost looks back in 12 at "no poem of mine extant", and takes cold comfort from the fact that his entry in Dunbar 'confirms/ our transient existence and that of our verse,/ the whilk (for a spell at least) made readers rejoice" (*Ghosts* 70), we recognise a familiar theme. In the course of the sequence, more than one figure of invention finds congenial air in historic cultural space: the ghost in 12 also records "that the Scots and English first tilted/ at fute-ball at Bewcastle, Cumberland, in 1599", which has been a passion with Conn for many a long year.

It becomes evident, then, that Edinburgh's first modern Makar took the opportunity of his tour of duty to extend the work of making in ways that develop patterns of self-construction present in his poetry early and late. After the 'Royal Mile' sequence establishes his contemporary credentials as an Edinburgh recorder, 'Roull of Corstorphin' imagines an historical genealogy for his continuing presence. While the notion of writing as an attempt to fix in language a world of flux and change is a commonplace, Conn brings into focus Scottish particularities of identity and relationship that belong to a wider story. For a son of the manse who never joined his father's church, poetry and art more generally come to serve as a necessary compensation for life's brevity. Given Conn's acceptance that mortality rounds every life with a bourne from which no traveller returns, it nonetheless seems reasonable to suggest that a "Presbyterian divine sermonising on sin" left his mark on a humanist son still committed to valorising the way we live. Christian metaphysics form no apparent part of the son's poetry, but the civilising ethic of its social gospel constitutes a significant part of the tradition from which he shapes his individual talent. Art is the only consolation we have.

"We are on borrowed time, you and I", is how the last poem in Conn's 1987 collection *At the Kibble Palace* ends, "And have been from the outset. All that is left, is to live lovingly" (110). That is either an almighty cop-out or a truth as difficult to practise as it was when a son of Galilee sought to persuade his Stone-Age listeners. Carving an ethic out of seizing the day, and driven to seek out and inscribe the instantaneous in a realm of possibility where time's trace is defined by its irretrievable passage into oblivion, Conn's lyric gift is constantly on the search for "a charging of nerve-ends/ too rapid to track" (*SP* 168), and as constantly drawn to painting in the effort to hold on to the stolen light of momentary perception. Perhaps that is why his often vivid lyricism is characteristically tinged with elegiac reflection, hedged with a sense of regret.

When a group of young back-packers jump off a train near Loch Lomond, the speaker of a poem called 'Faces' notes in their expression an "expectancy/ I'd all but given up on", and seeks to incorporate their glimpsed features in a consoling frame as "easy to visualise/ on Quattrocento canvases:/ his the gaze of a Giorgione/ shepherd-boy, that girl's poise/ pure Botticelli. Elsewhere/ Raphael skin-tones" (*SP* 178). Where living perception is identified in past time and associated with dead artists, that almost throwaway 'elsewhere' catches the poignancy of an impression already vanishing in the instant of its catching, and we begin to understand why durable art-work and statuary figure so prominently in this verse. At his best Conn matches the effect he praises in Iain Crichton Smith's "capturing of human trembling". "Thanks to you", he writes in 'Letters to Iain', "we see/ things differently, more acutely" (*SP* 190).

Note: interwoven into this article are excerpts from an extensive interview with Stewart Conn at his home in Fettes Row, Edinburgh, in May 2005, conducted by Colin Nicholson

Stewart Conn

Arthur's Seat Revisited

Early February. I am climbing on my own,
uncumbered by summer's ghosts. Below
are the slopes where my sons, when
young, used to go prancing and tumbling

or we'd bring holiday visitors to stretch
their legs. Today, none of the encircling hills
visible through cloud, the Castle and St Giles
could be from a store of etchings. On the crags

opposite a man shouts and whistles, the delay
making him seem idiotically out of synch
as he puffs and calls; the dog wisely or unwisely
keeping a low profile. Halfway down, aware

of an increasing pressure on my bladder
(combination of age and a drop in temperature)
I push my way gingerly into a gorse bush
to relieve myself; then rejoin the beaten track

only to realise I've left a small cloud of steam,
dissipating. I walk on, with on the skyline
a ring of painters, no doubt Breughels to a man,
waiting for the loch to freeze, ice to form.

At the Queen's Hall

Brahms: Sonata in G for piano and violin Op 78

When the rain so gently falleth,
Bygone dreams it still recalleth,
Fancies wild of childhood dreaming,
Through the sand when rain was streaming.
– Klaus Groth tr. EM Traquair

She sits in the front of the gallery, eyes closed, sparse
hair catching the light, head tilted as the melody soars,
on her features a wistfulness that is almost beatific.

Can these young musicians guess what they evoke
in older members of their audience, survivors from
a vanished age, its courtesies and etiquette long gone

and with them many a loved one – yet pursuing their lives
with something of a flourish? A smile now playing
at her lips, does she recall castles in the air, one-piece

swim-suits and ices (she buys one at the interval)
or girlish pranks in the dorm, moonlit escapades, kisses
stolen under parasols, prior to decades of self-sacrifice,

then loss? If so such poignancy in her re-emergence,
the applause dying, time no longer in abeyance
(the one reassurance, that high whine not her hearing-aid).

We come out to the din of the city, which absorbs all.
As we are crossing South Clerk Street we see her,
smudged features transformed … walking head in air.

Lion

granite carving by Ronald Rae

Its fine marriage of muscularity and grace
first envisaged at Tillyfourie Quarry
where the workers claimed they could trace
in it an animal's imprint, this 20-tonne block

of Corrennie granite, transported to Cramond,
was worked on for over a year, the sculptor
inspired as never before, seeing in this
a gift from the gods, the high-point of his career.

Now regal brow and mane, curved
flank, rippling haunch and great paw
have been invested by hammer and chisel
with the spirit and dignity of Lion.

Symbolic energy source, its roseate
stippling vibrant in sun or rain, how fit
to front our new Parliament – looking out
on Arthur's Seat, that other lion couchant.

Early Morning

You know the feeling – when rising early
and about to start work you become aware

of a distraction: not the customary
juddering of an adjoining water system,

shift of masonry behind the panelling,
nursery rhymes through the wall;

more a slightly asthmatic snoring,
but mellifluous and in perfect rhythm.

Has an inner partition been taken down,
some somnambulist moved in?

I throw open the shutters, let light in.
There they are on the garden wall,

the male cooing like a benign steam engine,
the females all a-do. A rap on the pane

and they've gone, clumsily as befits the elderly.
Next morning they're back, amorous as ever.

This time I leave them in peace. Worse things
to have outside your window than so decorous a love-in.

Musée d'Orsay

A slim figure in gold lamé
and a Tutenkhamen mask,
she bows stiffly each time
a coin is placed before her.

Inside, the Saison Anglais:
Burne-Jones maidens, *faïences*
by William Morris whose wife
gorged oysters with Rossetti –

his Lizzie disinterred, tresses
still growing, his sonnets having
to be doused in disinfectant
before he could read them.

More wholesome, Renoir's young
girl, wide-eyed amidst the dancers
and straw-hats of 'Le Moulin de la Galette':
such spontaneous *joie-de-vivre* ...

To think time has consumed all.
Under the station clock in the main hall
I cower lest a great locomotive come surging,
enveloping viewed and viewer in billows of steam.

Poetry Spring

Arctic hare and common stoat
in spring discard their winter coat,

having unlike other animals been
resplendent in blue fur and ermine.

This is not to be à la mode,
but to survive on life's harsh road.

So poets should not follow fashion,
but trust to their instinct and passion.

And if asked what they are at
say more ways than one, to skin a cat.

Storyteller

for Donald Smith

He told of snapping twigs and a crackling
in the undergrowth, followed by stillness
as King and Bear confronted each other.

Taking aim, the King released his bow-string.
In the moment between the arrow penetrating
the animal's breast and its collapsing, their

glances met. Something chilling the King's
blood he rushed home without his attendants,
decreeing that never again must a Bear be slain

in his domain. Hearing the story, those listening
had no need to ask what the Bear stood for.
It was there, deep inside each of them, hurting.

Autumn Visit: Barcelona

The tree-lined boulevards are broad as I remember,
the Barri Gòtic teeming as ever. But over the panoply
of flower-sellers and human statues there is a pall,
even the bustling Boqueria lacking interest compared

to when wide-eyed you strolled from stall to stall
choosing fruit and cheeses for our picnics; or returning
from the Palau de la Música we winked conspiratorially
at the statue of Marià Fortuny along from our hotel.

Even the season seems diluted, the colours less vibrant;
so that lest it lose its magic, the Parc Güell I regretfully
dismiss from my itinerary. For none of these deficiencies
do I blame the city… yours simply the spirit it lacks.

Couplet

Two writers agree that the prize doesn't
matter: one has won it, the other hasn't.

Fragrances

When visiting the nurse, I apply
your scented soap to my upper arm
and shoulder, put on a clean shirt,
for fear I'll offend with body-odours.

Before this evening's poetry reading,
clean-shaven, I liberally apply *Tuscany
per uomo*, hoping that my audience
will savour its spicy fragrance.

Yet going through daily life with you
who are closest in all the world, I don
no such finery, but simply take for granted
that you'll tolerate my company.

Cycle Runs

Hitting the kerb as I near Bilston Station,
my front wheel jolts: I almost lose
my grip on the handlebars. This happens

again crossing a play area where boys
on mountain-bikes doing acrobatic wheelies
threaten to go head over heels.

It brings back times when cycling up
to the farm on misty autumn mornings
I passed where a wild-eyed stallion shied

at an invisible object in mid-air,
then crumpled, nostrils foaming, splayed
hooves flailing. A prickle of fear

makes me wonder why – and wonder too
at the vulnerability of us all to the little
it can take, to overthrow the mind.

The Challenge

The challenge with art, as with life,
  lies in holding it together;

in keeping your flotilla of paper boats
  afloat, the deeper the waters you explore.

Or put another way: the purer the note,
  the greater the fear the glass will shatter.

Piping to Stewart's Tune

John Sampson

The last piece of writing I was asked to do was ten years ago when I did a piece for the Salvation Army on the evolution of the trumpet. To communicate how Stewart and I collaborated on Roull of Corstorphin, a mediaeval poet celebrated as "gentill Roull" in William Dunbar's famous poem 'The Lament for the Makaris', set in the early part of the 16th century, for so august a periodical as *Chapman* is much more daunting.

Stewart and I got chatting after I'd played at a Brian McCabe book launch, reminiscing over the days when I worked for him as a composer during his time as Head of BBC Radio Drama in the early 1980s. He mentioned that he was finishing a set of poems about Roull and wondered if I would be interested in providing music to link the poems at the readings he had been invited to give at various societies and festivals.

I was intrigued, and when I read them I realised that there was scope for musical punctuation but was all too aware that the writing was beautifully crafted and began to wonder if there was a need to add anything at all! He convinced me otherwise by pointing out that music from the 16th century would be made appropriate by using authentic sounds from instruments of the period such as the cornett, crumhorn, shepherd's pipe and the voices of recorders from garklein to bass to bring to it as much musical colour as possible. My main concern when responding to a text is to find the right music to integrate with the words so as to set an atmosphere by providing connecting links between segments, or, when appropriate, a poetic underscore running beneath the words.

In 1979 I was asked by director John Carnegie to compose music for *Hecuba*, a play by Stewart based on Euripides to underline its relevance to our times with its racist doctrines and human miseries – especially genocide. This was our first collaboration, and the experience was stimulating and creative; there were two successful runs at the Traverse and the production toured Scotland with Winged Horse Theatre Company.

The following year he invited me to be musical director on William Grant's play *Swansong* which was part of the BBC/Arts Council of Great Britain scheme for new work in theatre. The music was mostly specified by Grant and included songs not only in Scots but also in Gaelic. As I had never worked for radio drama before, Stewart instructed me about the lengths of tunes sustainable in broadcast and where and when voice-over would be appropriate. He also made suggestions on vocal and instrumental arrangements, and musical 'arguments' – which I duly followed and found his advice to be in tune with Grant's intuitions about his play.

His intuitive understanding of text and music comes from the fact that he is one of Scotland's leading playwrights with credits such as *The*

Stewart Conn and a 'Blast from the Past' – John Sampson

Burning, *Herman* and *The Aquarium* (for which I also did the music in a dramatised reading). *Swansong* was produced at Perth Rep and broadcast on Radio 3. He then pointed me in the direction of others in his department and I went on to do many other plays – thanks to him.

Choosing music for *Roull* was a collaborative process. To link the last line from 'At Court': "he will sit penning his tender love poetry", I suggested 'Bonnie Sweet Robin' by Antony Holborne as it's very gentle, and playing it on the tenor recorder linked to his next poem which starts with the line: "I retain mellow memories of your visit". At the end of this poem about his cousin in 'Aberdene' he, with a touch of humour, said "What about 'The Northern Lights of Old Aberdeen'? The Crumhorn beckoned. We found it amusing to have an anachronistic piece of music played on a 16th Century instrument, giving a quirky texture it was unlikely ever to have had before. Scotland has a great tradition of composers and music from this period. One of our unsung heroes is Robert Carver (1485-c1568) and I was able to find the music for 'L'Homme Armé', a piece adapted (or as the poet puts it, 'usurped' by Carver) to place under a section of poetry relating to the composer, to add authority to the underscore. It's all the more appropriate because the sequence mentions Scone, where Carver trained as an Augustinian canon, and, specifically, how "the radiance of singing in the Chapel Royal touched the heart strings, transfiguring them with his interweaving harmonies".

For 'Insomnia', Stewart recommended something slow, to be there for the duration of the poem. In that mediaeval period, music was written in individual polyphonic and intermingled parts, unlike modern music which is structured around chordal harmony. So I came up with an improvised piece based on a Carver theme from his great mass. For Stewart's poem 'In Seikness', which ends with the words "the ghaistly cock sall craw", a soft, gentle piece of French 16th century music called 'Belle Qui Tiens Ma Vie' played on the bass recorder created the right atmosphere to lead into 'Roull on Death'.

It's such a asset to Scottish culture in general that John Purser brought off his enormous 'coup' in *Scotland's Music*, the radio series (30 episodes, 90 minutes each!) and, in the book of the same name, a point of reference for both Stewart and myself. It's a musical bible, establishing once and for all just how intrinsically musical this Scottish nation is.

Having started the Roull cycle on the cornettino (a bright brass-sounding instrument with woodwind fingering) it felt right to finish this bright sound with 'La Mourisque' by Tylman Surato (1500-1561).

With the music in place and instrumentation agreed, Stewart came up with the notion that I should wear early 16th century costume while he remained in neutral black 21st century mode. This was the hook I needed: I began to see myself as the ghost from the period who arrives to play the music which would have a legitimate place within the poems.

Before we unleashed this collaboration to an unsuspecting public we needed to try it out on someone. Who better than Judy, Stewart's wife, who was summoned from the kitchen to be an audience of one! We performed for her at full power, in costume, in their living room where the words and the instruments rattled the four corners of the room. Judy warmed to our efforts and assured us enthusiastically that we were ready for 'the real thing'. Armed with her approval, we went on to perform the work at the National Library of Scotland, the Stirling Poetry Society and the Edinburgh Book Festival. EBF is wonderful to be part of and, as I stood outside the studio tent straining to hear the cue for my entrance in tights, feathered cap and sequined gown, I got some strange looks from workmen. Perhaps they thought I was a ghost! Or something else!

It was a great sight to see so many people as I entered playing my two recorders and to see Stewart's smile as I made my way to the platform. We had fun with the piece, but never to the detriment of the words – which remained sacrosanct. The audience were warm in their response and Stewart, who is a wonderful interpreter of his own work, made the words seem as fresh and vibrant as the day they were written.

As his 70th birthday passes, drink a toast to him and Judy, and wish them both long life and eternal happiness.

We so enjoy working together because both of us can be inventive as to how the music is used, both prominently and atmospherically. The collaboration works on a level of total perfectionism and professionalism, stimulating each other to greater activity and achievement – and always with the sole aim of achieving the best for the work. I find always that we arrive at the end product in total agreement. I look forward to working with him again on an equally interesting project, as I remind him of Nietsche's quote: "Life without music would be a mistake".

Anda Paterson, Shrove Tuesday *(continued on page 111)*

Authors' Ghosts: Muriel Spark, the Poet

Stewart Conn

From early in their careers James Kennaway and Muriel Spark were bracketed as writers in whose work Scottish origins could be traced, though both had already spent most of their lives out of the country. A destructive manipulator is, as it happens, central to his *Household Ghosts*, as it is to her *The Prime of Miss Jean Brodie* (both published in 1961). An *en passant* comparison between them provides a convenient springboard.

In 1965 I commissioned Kennaway to write a radio play. In due course he broke his flight back from the States where he'd been discussing a film with Rex Harrison, to stop over in Glasgow for the read-through. He kept scribbling on his script-envelope what I assumed were notes for the cast. No, he said, he'd been working out how much it was costing him a minute just to sit there. Over coffee he asked if I wrote. I confessed I was completing a first book of poems. He replied disdainfully that any real writer could dash off that sort of thing on the side, if he could be bothered. I don't think he ever did. Tragically, he was killed in a car-crash three years later.

Introducing her poems of six decades, Spark's was a very different stance: "Although most of my life has been devoted to fiction, *I have always thought of myself as a poet.* I do not write 'poetic' prose, but feel that my outlook on life and my perceptions of events are those of a poet." Adding that "for creative writing of any sort, an early apprenticeship as a poet is a wonderful stimulant and start".

At eleven she was "discovering the delights of poetry and art through that wonderful teacher Christina Kay ... There was a small writing-desk in my grandmother's room for me to use while I was minding her. It had a sloping leather-covered surface which opened flat, and numerous drawers for papers and secrets. I was always happy at a desk. There, while my grandmother dozed, I did my homework, wrote my poems, read the books that I had brought home from the public library earlier in the evening and wrote letters, usually to my best friend Frances Niven with whom I shared our schoolroom double desk. Frances wrote letters to me; we would exchange them next day. We neither of us had a telephone in the house. Our letters were comments on the poetry we were reading or on ideas for our nature studies." (*Curriculum Vitae*, pp 90 & 95)

She continues: "My poetry was rather more sophisticated than my prose. I was deeply interested in rhythms and curious about what one could make them mean in poetry. My Poem 'The Gallop' did indeed speed over the pages for five stanzas." Here is a sample, its double-stressed lines gathering momentum:

Horses wild horses!
Alive as they gallop

In fury along!
As they gallop and gallop
And gallop along!
And gathering speed,
And faster and faster,
Nor heeding disaster,
All trying to lead.
And breathing is strong
As they gallop along,
As they gallop and gallop along … (*CV* p 97-98)

The theme is not uncommon with young girls. But she had another compelling interest: "I was reading the Border ballads so repetitively and attentively that I memorised many of them without my noticing it. The steel and bite of the ballads, so remorseless and yet so lyrical, entered my literary bloodstream, never to depart." [*CV* p 98] When 14 she was crowned at the 1932 Scottish Ideal Homes Exhibition for "the best poem commemorating the death of Sir Walter Scott" – further strands interweaving.

Of Bulawayo in the early 40s, her unhappy marriage already over, she reveals: "All this time I had never stopped writing poetry. I entered twice for the Rhodesian poetry competition and won twice. One of the poems was called 'The Go-Away Bird', about the haunting cry of the grey-crested lourie." (*CV*, p 135) Years later she gave the title to a short story. Her first book of poems *The Fanfarlo* was published in 1952; a story keeping the title piece's central character won the *Observer* Short Story Competition; and her first novel *The Comforters* came out in 1957. The rest, as they say, would be literary history.

My brief and pleasurable contacts with Muriel Spark were through adapting and directing *Jean Brodie* for radio, and being given free rein to abridge and broadcast other novels and stories – the former including *A Far Cry from Kensington* and *Symposium*, read by Eleanor Bron with a glacial panache of which the author approved. I met her only once, in the Edinburgh Arts Club, when she received honorary membership of Scottish PEN. Her 'private' self I've glimpsed only via the autobiographical *Curriculum Vitae* with its lacerating put-downs and settling of scores from her days at The Poetry Society and editing *Poetry Review*.

All the Poems (2004) contains a score of additions to the *Collected Poems I* of 1968. Rather than try to span these here I'll focus on one or two of the seven poems comprising *Authors' Ghosts* – chosen, arranged and published in a limited edition by David Rees and Angus O'Neill who "did of course run both selection and sequence past Muriel for her approval".

Instantly detectable are the often-enigmatic observations, aural patterns, strict metrical expertise and constant undercurrents of unease I think of as among her hallmarks. By one of those uncanny coincidences, only a few days before becoming aware of the edition, I'd sent off to my publisher the manuscript of what became my own most recent collection, *Ghosts at Cockcrow,* its title chosen for its tremors of transience, and its echoing of the world of the ballads.

Spark's title poem draws us right from the start ("I think that authors' ghosts creep back/ Nightly to haunt the sleeping shelves") into an inner world, riding on the continued sonority of those **o** and double-**o** vowels. A subsequent interjection ("But was it like that?/ I don't remember this") and ellipsis are not simply the equivalent of a musical break, but combine to convey a tremulousness presaging what follows. By the end ("... something's missing – I could have sworn ...") not only have the tables been turned but there is, in the querulous tapering away of that final line, the disconcerting implication (as I read it) that the frailty of memory is not the author's but that of the speaker, or reader.

'Created and Abandoned' which begins "Where have you gone, how has it ended with you,/ people of my dreams, cut off in mid-life, gone to the grave?" again unravels onion-layers to reveal hidden depths. The Dreamer is analogous to an Author who, having created the characters, abandons them on wakening (completing the book?). Intriguing are both the 'handicapped' or stunted nature of those virtually rendered ghosts, and the sympathy afforded them. The poem ends on a dual note of concern for their welfare and of responsibility toward them, as night after night they may be fruitlessly waiting. Is the final "Are you all right?" a twinge of guilt? And this in an author more accustomed in her fiction to manipulate her characters with the precision of a jewelled wrist-watch ... and often with something of an icicle at her heart.

The first of these poems dates from 2003, the latter from about 1979. Her own patterning of the *Collected Poems* flagrantly disregards chronology, allowing one to compare the poems and to try to date them. Early ones have a crisp metric and formal orderliness (if at times, as in 'The Ballad of the Fanfarlo', something of the obscurantism of the period), and often a sting in the tail. Later poems are looser-limbed and more conversational. But all display a penetrating poise, strictness of form, a sharp wit, and at times a sense of fun. Even these amusing poems, though, can depict solitariness, not just in people but in one instance a forlorn single shoe, as in 'The Lonely Shoe Lying on the Road':

> One sad shoe that someone has probably flung
> out of a car or truth. Why only one? ...
> That one shoe in the road invokes
> my awe and my sad pity.

I like her best where most succinct, and where the poems embody (as do so many of the novels) those qualities encapsulated in 'The Empty Space' (2002). Again a ghost is conjured up: this time of a painting. It is of the view seen from the window of the room in which it hangs: the umbrous milieu round Castel S Angelo, "guardian of old Rome". The word 'guardian' has a fine nuance. For the poem's brief narrative brings an ominous transformation: its last line reads, "It is all over now. The thieves came by night".

This poem also strikes in me a subjective chord. First visiting Rome three decades ago I stayed in Monte Mario with a translator friend Franca Violani and her husband Ettore, who collected old paintings, and was restoring a Bassano landscape. I'd never been in an apartment more copiously locked and bolted. Over my bed in an oval frame was a Madonna once attributed to Leonardo (supposedly of the same model as his 'Virgin of the Rocks'). In a poem I record being unable to sleep, due to the whining of a mosquito; and the exquisite dilemma when it at last settled, precisely on the nose of the Madonna.

In her preface to the *Collected Poems* Spark further claims: "Whether in prose or verse, all creative writing is mysteriously connected with music and I always hope this factor is apparent throughout my work." She has a flawless ear – think of (most appropriately) her 'Verlaine Villanelle' – for both the modulation of a line and repetition of a phrase, and a strangely 'singing' quality reminiscent of that early love of the ballads which struck her for their savagery as well as their clarity. And for that mix of fantasy and reality, brought out hauntingly in the radio version of an early novel dominated by Dougal Douglas, MA (Edin), in which "the lion howls, and the devil prowls, in the streets of Peckham Rye".

At the 2004 Edinburgh Book Festival Spark spoke much of memory – and of forgetting. The writer in her would seem to have had little difficulty 'remembering': whether locations, encounters, or the gossamer intricacies often central to her plots and characters. Given her age, too – the occasion was not so long before her death earlier this year at 88 – she spanned cataclysmic real-life worlds of social and cultural change.

I'll end on a personal footnote, and with another time-shift. In 'Everything Plus The Kitchen Sink', the one poem in the limited edition not from *All the Poems*, a friend of Spark's in New York sounds a friend in Rome for news of her (for a biography?). It refers to her home in Trastevere. On that first visit of mine, I was taken to visit an artist called Zev, who lived near the Tiber. Of Native American origin but self-exiled from the States, his apartment was an Aladdin's cave. On display were silver goblets for the king of Saudi Arabia. And he told me he was under commission to make a jewel-cabinet for a near neighbour who was away at the time, on holiday or in Tuscany: Muriel Spark.

Zev's motif was a half-moon. I bought my wife one as a pendant – and a smaller one for myself, which I still wear. Zev must be long dead. I'd love to know if Muriel Spark ever got the jewel-chest. By way of a metaphor, her output could be seen as a hoard of riches. It is the novels and stories which have, rightly, been universally lauded. But I see the pick of her poems as gems, glinting and fine-facetted, within the copiously encrusted coffer of her opus as a whole. My own pick would be those revealing her, often tantalisingly, as a mistress of disquiet; poems which tread thin ice, and hint – her *aperçus* the more unsettling for their lightness of touch, their avoidance of solemnity – at chill depths; at the precariousness of our lives, at our hopes and frailty, loneliness and loss – those verities, which are part of the true poet's domain.

And I still see, imprinted in the woman who wrote them, the very lively ghost of a young girl, hunched at her grandmother's writing-desk, from which wild horses couldn't tear her.

(a revised version of a talk delivered at the annual lunch of the Muriel Spark Society on Sunday 30 January 2005, in the Bruntsfield Hotel, Edinburgh. Author's Ghosts, 7 Poems by Muriel Spark, *was edited and published by David Rees and Angus O'Neill, London, 2004.)*

Ministrations

The ghosts who haunt us
are not those who belong
to our superstitious past

or to childhood fancy,
gliding unconcernedly
through solid walls, clanking

chains in dank corridors
or descending stairways,
their heads in their arms.

Equally white-vestured
they are the apparitions
who will rise ahead of us

bearing pills and bedpans,
holding our hands
in unfamiliar rooms;

in gauze masks attending
during the operation,
helping to alleviate pain;

then when the day comes
drawing the sheet finally
over our flaccid faces.

Upon which it is we
who will dissolve, not they.
Best believe in them.

from *Ghosts at Cockcrow*, (Bloodaxe Books, 2005)

In the Fun-House of Stewart Conn's Cortex

Kevin T McEneaney

Since there's no money in rhyme (celebrity exceptions give no guarantee of quality), poets muddle on from poem to poem, book to book, without anyone but close friends noticing their scribbling. If a poet manages a *Selected*, an honest examination by new readers can induce mild shock or vertigo – where did this guy come from; why haven't I heard of him?

Such was the effect on me of Conn's *Stolen Light* (*Selected Poems*, Bloodaxe, 1999, (*SP*)). Here was a poet of range and unfaltering technique, fully equipped with a travel-light palette, offering an engaging Montaigne-like gaze into the mirror of identity, providing truly stimulating landscapes, travelogues and meditations. I'm not fond of the hortatory mode and am noted for acerbic asides on incompetence and narcissism in that merchandising madhouse which passes for literature. But diligent trolling through muck and gravel eventually produces that contagious excitement when one discovers a diamond in compensation for the hours or weeks of boredom that afflict industrious readers.

So what light has Conn stolen? He's filched an identity from the *samsara* of illusion that floods literary trends. He's taken his own path up the foggy mountain, experimenting with techniques, self-examinations, and rhythms as he exudes charm. He's not hiding under some magisterial cloak of a muck-a-muck high priest – but is at home in his own skin. Early poems may have been influenced by Dylan Thomas and later poems by W H Auden, but he has relegated those influences to the background, just as Thomas did with John Clare and Auden did with Samuel Coleridge.

Nature remains the bedrock test for any poet (and here 20th century Anglo-Scots poetry has excelled) because Nature supplies both the most universal theme – our mortality in the cosmos – and provides poets with the largest vocabulary available, no matter the native tongue. Conn's early poems explore the personalities of an older generation immured in the great womb of Nature: the raising of animals, hunts, and sympathetic eulogy for the quirky humanity of a generation that didn't give a fig for the onslaught of technology. Devoid of Thomas's nostalgia and rhetoric, Conn limns earthy portraits that dramatise their tragedy, his technique and perspective closer to Thomas Hardy than Dylan Thomas. His ear has more modern nuance: his rhymes and half-rhymes have a casual, near-invisible quality, while the Ayrshire personalities he records are as vivid as those etched in Patrick Kavanagh's Monaghan. Now that this rural generation who knew Nature and its indifference to the annals of human history has vanished, we can better appreciate what Conn has done for neighbours like Todd and the region at large. Subsequently, he moves to a leaner, more urbane line, varying in length and characterised by more explosive alliteration, as in his poems about Shetland ponies:

They clatter and jolt,
are pluff-bellied, biff
posts, thrum their trough
with warm breathing, smelt

ice. On the skyline (*SP* 34)

This minimalist approach chisels landscape with an austere beauty; a playfully reflective voice emerges as in 'Under Creag Mhor' where he appropriates a worn topic and transforms it into something interesting. This looks easy until you try it: the lochs "pleated with clear water,/ no longer house dinosaur/ and plated myth." (*SP* 33) The use of 'plated myth', indicates both the etiolating of formulaic myth and the historical reference to the Scythian Alans whose dragon-fish-scale platted armour brutalised the Scottish landscape for centuries along Hadrian's wall, resulting in the fantastic myth of the dragon under water. The last line about the sunning lizard, that "such monsters huddle yet", unexpectedly updates the myth to humankind's perennial fear of subjugation and oppression, and this reversal reifies the wisdom of popular folklore.

Conn's use of metaphors often breezily carries such compact freighting that their giant dimensions may be overlooked. He now feels comfortable using any line length. His landscape poetry becomes more intimately wedded to family and friends; he confesses the impulse that impels him to write poetry: "the thought of what loved-ones may suffer" ('Before Dark' *SP* 74). Such selfless concern may not resonate with a generation bent on exhibitionism, but how can we dismiss such empathy for others? There are eloquent poems about children (see 'Two Poems' *SP* 77-9) that exude a charm any father would cherish.

Turning to autobiography, Conn begins contemplating art in public and in the privacy of his study. More formally, he's concerned with the tension between mortality and aesthetics ('In the Gallery' *SP* 84), but informally explores the world of the artist in the face of social disaster ('Recovery' *SP* 99), concluding that the really great forces in life are "endurance and love". (*SP* 100) He meditates on the treasures of public art while he paints portraits of friends and self-portraits. The final poem in this section, 'Springtime', yokes public and private as he gazes on the portrait of a young girl: "All that is left, is to live lovingly". This echoes Auden's last line of 'September 1, 1939', but stands in its own right as the final statement in an impressive gallery. Conn never descends to the garrulous prolixity that later afflicted Auden, and achieves an intimacy Auden could never accomplish. He offers several short sequences: a painting by Renoir, poems about Skye, a visit to an acquaintance, and the unicorn tapestries at the Cloisters in Manhattan.

In this *agon* between Nature and art, Nature emerges clear winner, though that may not be Conn's intention. The poems on art display wit, invention, and imagination, yet I'm more excited by the thrifty language on birds in Skye. His sketches of the French countryside are more immediate and vital than his considered meditations on art in France, picnicking in Provence or bicycling in the Garonne – these are compelling and lively. But the leaner lines at Skye are more plosively packed with alliteration and clearly he is more in his element. The final poem of 'October Week' effectively conveys the conceit that we are all guests on shifting tectonic plates; the pan-Celticism evoked becomes a metaphor for the greater human family on this fragile globe. If taken as a series, these poems dramatise how a return home from wanderings refreshes the familiar.

All poets are rebels to some degree, but only a rebel can create what's new. Conn's rebellion remains civilised and subtle. at its root rebellion his displacement of church for the world of art. This explains his obsessive need to meditate on the textures of art and how people respond to these, for he's not solely concerned with his own responses. It is the choir of artists who reveal the world's luminosity to us, devoid of any philosophy, directed only by the open heart, and in this sense he's a questing prophet inquiring into the motivations behind the creation of art, nowhere more so than in his latest book, *Ghosts at Cockcrow (*Bloodaxe, 2005 (*GC*).

The title of his book of miscellaneous prose, *Distances (*Scottish Cultural Press, 2001) refers not only to a range of geographical places (Scotland, South Africa, America, Spain), but also to how artists (mostly Scottish poets and sculptors he's known) cope with the exile of distance that art imposes upon the creator. He brings a critical eye to his modest experiences; his honesty insures authenticity even when he's grappling with his own embarrassments like a fishhook in his finger ('Off the Water', *GC* 91) or the daft feeling of irrelevancy at growing old ('Autumn Walk', *GC* 38). He puts himself unflinchingly under the microscope *and* has a real talent for public portraiture, as in 'Survivor' (*SP* 150) and 'Letters to Iain' (*SP* 187-92). He has of late written some enduring public poems like 'The Holy City' (*GC* 22-3), on the bombing of Clydebank, and 'The Emigrants' with its deftly ironic conclusion (*GC* 27-8); also, 'Footage of RLS' (GC 43) where he expertly uses the technique of rush-footage snippets, leaving the resurrected ghost of Robert Louis Stevenson smiling enigmatically after the show.

Ghosts at Cockcrow is marvellous for the range and perfection of so many poems, especially the masterpiece 'Roull of Corstorphin'. To anyone who has dabbled in 16th century prose and poetry, the ambiance of the poems conjures a pleasing frisson between 16th century and contemporary usage. The historical poem has been the graveyard of many poets – a galaxy of talents in the 20th century failed at it: David Jones, William Carlos Williams, Charles Olson, to name a few. In most cases, the very size of their canvas and voracious ambition doomed these projects, while more concise historical sequences have endured: Eliot's

Wasteland, Pound's *Hugh Selwyn Mauberly*, Kavanagh's *The Great Hunger*, MacDiarmid's *A Drunk Man*, John Montague's *The Rough Field*, Ted Hughes's *Moortown* and Brendan Kennelly's *Cromwell*. The more successful approaches to sequence appropriate either place or personality, as with MacDiarmid or the prolix folkloric personality of Kennelly.

Conn has chosen a specific personality that has vanished and has relocated that personality strictly within historical confines, imitating 16th-century stanza techniques with effortless expertise. William Dunbar in 'Lament for the Makars' calls Roull of Corstorphin "gentill" and this allows Conn to employ Roull, the first recorded poet of Edinburgh, as foil to the goliardic flyting antics of the era, vesting him with an urbane civility characteristic of Conn himself. This provides a doubled image while creating a myth of an Ur-poet, civilised in inclinations and sensibilities, holding up harmony in music as the fundamental ideal for community. The doubling motif of making Roull of Aberdene a cousin continues an echoing chain that turns almost choral. Above all, Roull is portrayed as healer-poet, offering a cure for insomnia (such poems are universal in folkloric roots), and the gift of love to his aging wife. The portrayal of Roull as environmentalist may seem out of tune, but poets have traditionally held trees to be sacred, lamenting their destruction as desecration of the poetic impulse, especially in the Celtic heritage.

Roull is no saint, as his quest for fame promotes his narcissism at court, yet his lament for the loss of his poems to posterity remains more a lament for the human transience of empires and civilisation itself. The populist postscript petition by barber-surgeons underscores by contrast how differently Roull was distanced from his own times; combating horror (plague here) with humour has always been the universal strategy of both lower classes and upper classes. The suggestion that a lower class sport, football, is ruining social health and that it be replaced by an upper-class sport, archery, is a cunning invitation for the lower classes to perfect the art of poaching on the land-rich estates of the nobility. Roull offers personal solutions to living life more fully, while the guild of barber-surgeons jestingly proposes turning the social order upside down in the name of public health. From a modern perspective the jest is outrageous, especially if we recall, with a tinge of horror, that Scotland's most accomplished poet, Lord Byron, died from the barber-surgeon's art of bleeding.

The Roull sequence presents a meditation on the poet's role in society: Roull is active at court, but is more committed to domestic and local life; he has the goodness that Dunbar singles out, but lacks Dunbar's vitriolic rhetorical grace, and the gritty wit of the flyter Kennedy. Conn's argument is more realistic and limited, as one would expect in any post-modern meditation. The upper classes tend to equate poetry with self-conscious cleverness while writing about the ego or items of ownership, while the lower classes opt for emotional thrust and political rhetoric.

Conn's poetry exhibits neither extremes. At times he may appear overly-obsessed with museum art but he's not interested in explaining art in an academic manner. He's interested in the common humanity evoked by the artist and how music or painting reaches out into our private lives in 'Piazza del Campidoglio' (*GC* 88-9); poems like 'In the Museum of Scotland' (*GC* 75) illustrate the interconnectedness of public and private artifacts and dreamscape. Conn is never an escapist (art for art's sake), but a contemplative searcher for the humane aspects of life: generosity, love, friendship, social conscience, and the gentle humour that unites all. This remains true whether he considers Goya, football, hiking up a hill, family relations, animals, or portraits of others – and in the last I find a varied approach in technique different from the miniature sonnet portraits perfected by Ford Maddox Ford and continued by Robert Lowell and Seamus Heaney ('In Memory of Robert Fitzgerald'). Like any true poet, Conn is *un autre* in Arthur Rimbaud's phrase – an outsider, observing society, art, his life. And like any intellectual, he's not comfortable about what he observes when he peers more closely.

One of Conn's over-arching themes is that we habitually fail to notice the beauty that surrounds us, whether in landscape, art, or the virtues of individuals. Though he's not blind to difficulties, he's a firmly-grounded optimist who believes that cheer possesses healing qualities. He accomplishes this optimistic outlook not through preaching or rhetorical posturing, but restrained inference. This slant restraint gives energy to both his conscience and technique. He remains always resolutely himself, illustrating Walt Whitman's dictum that character "gives predominant stamp to advancing poetry" (preface to the centennial edition of *Leaves of Grass*). There's no vatic pretence or coy hermetic legerdemain here, but a civilised man trying to make sense of a world more pretentious than he, while mildly noting things like "The slow dereliction of Church and State" (from *The Luncheon of the Boating Party,* Bloodaxe, 1992, 10) in the increasingly brutalised world we inhabit. In the technique of rhyme, Anglo-Scots poetry has always dominated English poetry (Pope and Keats being exceptions), and Conn sits firmly anchored in this heritage accomplishing nuanced *frisson* in a seemingly effortless manner.

I'm struck by this because in America many poets don't have an ear; much American poetry buzzes flat as a voice overheard on Alexander Graham Bell's monstrous convenience. But if one pays attention to Conn's lines, one can only marvel at his craftsmanship. Not part of the braid tradition of Burns, MacDiarmid, and Matthew Fitt, he writes an international English with Scottish inflections, reaching a wider audience, calling attention to Scottish virtues in indirect ways: memorialising landscape, local characters with an identifiable Scots humour.

When it comes to criticism of poetry, the acid test is similar to a dram. Do I want another? Can I read, and more importantly, re-read a poem several times? Do I discover further depths to the thinking, more pleasure in the syntax, more resonance in sound? No theory or technique, no matter how lofty or expert, can rescue mediocre poetry. Much of the poetry I possess dwells in boxes down in my basement book hell, but I keep Stewart's books in my bedroom because I do my reading in bed (and most of my writing). I continually find refreshment in Stewart's work. I can read him at random with pleasure, delighted by his humane wisdom, amused by his puckish delight in discovering epiphanies of healing joy.

Roving in Zagreb

Eating horse with Stewart Conn
was a most civilized experience
as we spoke of civilization's decay
and the brutal way ambition
instigates dereliction
of the sincere heart beat
when true travellers meet.

Unless you're satiric like Homer,
anger and revenge can never
sound those high grace notes
that linger like blossoms and float
down the stream of memory,
multiplying joy and love
with spontaneous zest –
for example, Mozart.

A quiet, intimate moment
of shared contemplation
rooted in dialectic digression
like a swooping cormorant
contains the matrix of the matter.

Ambulation free of dispute
lies at the root
of who we are.

Who remembers the details
of heated disputation?
What we most treasure
remains the gentle auras
coalescing around an image:
whether that be opening an umbrella
to the spatter of hailstones,
or wandering down a blind alley
like Odysseus far from stony Ithaka.

Christine De Luca

For a New Decade of Song

for Stewart Conn

A biblical span, a decade ending; but Autumn
is your heady season, your sensation, when
twilight adds a grace note to life's music,
shifts discord in its plagal resolution. Now

time's measured by a gentle clock – light's rim,
the declination of a sun still bold. Watch
where her finger gilds your morning window
and where she lingers in her dipping cadence.

The year will turn, and an artist paint surreal
a landscape back-lit, impermanent; yield energy
flat-packed in brushstrokes, liquid long, with
stolen light drawn from marks and layering.

And you, with skill absurdly green, will conjure
flutes from treetops for a new decade of song.

(from *There's a Poem to be Made*)

David Betteridge

A Riddle

After Riddle 66 in The Exeter Book

Compared with the Moon, I am brighter;
compared with the Sun, swifter.
All oceans' heavy mass
and continents' far stretch of miles
I hold with ease.
Deep-diving under Hell,
high-soaring Heaven-ward and beyond,
I know each latest and most ancient inch and moment
of Space-Time; into them, and you,
giving of myself, I flow.
Greater in my magnitude than this
or any Universe,
yet I shrink as small as any living cell.

Say who you think I am. (You know.)

A Botany Lesson

A Canon in the Key of Gold

See the mature plant!
I tap its flowering shoot.
You'll see a little pollen shooting out
against this sheet of card.
Imagine now a field, and ripening sun,
a puff of pollen on a breeze,
caught somewhere by a second plant downwind,
welcoming it with feathery lures.

Then there's the meeting and a mating
with a stranger-friend,
a fall together and a perilous journey for a season
underground. Next arousing, and a rising;
and, with changing shape,
an entrance into the world of light.

It's here, a year on, at journey's end,
other shoots will flower,
and other puffs of pollen, epic gold,
will start their risky circumnavigation
of the year.

Climbing Beinn Dobhrain

In Praise of Duncan Ban MacIntyre

For Ronald Stevenson, who has recently completed
a choral and orchestral epic, Ben Dorain,
which celebrates the life and work of Duncan Ban MacIntyre.

A perfect cone –
that is how it seems from this direction
as we drive towards it from the south.
But suddenly Beinn Dobhrain's skewed –
the road has veered,
our line of vision shifts around.

Here's the way we'll climb:
to the midpoint of the saddle there,
that joins Beinn Dobhrain and its northern twin
Beinn a Duthaidh – then on beyond, south and back,
following the skyline's rocky ridge
until, like geometers, we stand
right on the cone's fine tip.
(It's the obvious route.)
The climate changes as we go:
in the valley bottom: Spring;
high up, an Arctic gale, perhaps;
and, like as not, some snow.

We need two kinds of mental set.
We're careful where we place our feet –
there's bog and boulder to contest,
and slippery grass and scree.
At all our frequent zigs and zags,
we need to bear in mind just where
we mean to be before the day is done.

(Writing this poem is the same:
the words reflect our fragile steps;
the finished work, the peak.)
We'll watch for mist.

When Duncan Ban was ghillie on these slopes
his quarry was the running deer;
but, as poet, like all who deeply think,
he looked for more than eyes alone can find.
The hunted squarely in his sights,
he found so many ways to lead a troop

of boisterous words
to quiet, rest, and home.

Listen: the music of the wind and water
and the occasional bird grows sharper, clearer, closer,

as we climb.
I think how much we've left behind
since setting out,
how much (not only height) we've gained …

We've reached – no, not quite,
not yet, a little further … and a little further still
– and now at last, the top!
It's powdered with a recent snow.
Good! The wind has freshened,
and blown away all mist and cloud.
Nothing overlooks or tops
except the blue umbrella of the sky.
The prospect from this peak,
as much as Chomalungma
or any massive mountain anywhere –
even Sinai or other sacred site –
for us, for while we're here,
is earth's best crown.
I think our vantage point could be,
has now become, a place
of sudden mela, mod and jamboree.
We're joined by poets
of all languages and times,
and Duncan Ban's their president.
It's not the wind's hum,
but the glory of these poets' words we hear.
They share their travels and travails;
life's truths and beauties; queries, quests;
things loved, things learned.
Our view of Scotland –
our view from Scotland –
broadens fast.

Great Ghillie,
and all other poets gathered here,
lead us on the upward curving
of your inspiration's track; show us
where our long-sought quarry lies.
(You know its many forms, its names,

the places where it ranges free, and hides.)
And, once our vision-hungry souls are filled,
through the pibroch of your words' unwinding,
surely, safely, homeward
bring us back.

Gifts for a Poet

If I fashion beauty ever,
others fashion me.
From a lineage that reaches far,
I take and use and learn.

From India:
a flute, a dead stick, cut and bored
with ancient skill.
It takes the silence of my breath
and breaks it, moulds it, and transforms it
on the slant of fipple, sounding edge, and fingerholes
and makes as many melodies
as time and inspiration will allow.
Its cost so small,
its potential, infinite.

From China:
a tangram, a square of paper
with five scissor lines; when cut,
seven shapes result.
I move them, varying the angle of their fit,
and summaries appear in hard-edged black
of worlds of three-dimensioned living fact.

From Japan:
a brush and ink.
In mind, if not in deed,
with fluent curvilinear strokes,
I paint no end of pictures,
each preserving in a perfect sweep of form
the essences of all I celebrate.

If I gain a glimpse of any truth,
it's from the legacy
that friends and world prepare.
Nothing is my own, and all is shared.

In the Garden

Julie Stradner

The man stumbles into the garden before dawn. For a moment he leans on the iron gate, stands panting and dry-mouthed. In front of him looms a plum tree, its fruit split and spilled over the wet grass. Wasps already glitter in the silver light. He shoves open the gate, stoops, scoops up the fruits and crams them into his mouth, licking the juice that runs over his fingers, his bleeding nails. Far off a dog barks and he jerks, freezes, stares off behind him at the ranks of maize, the stands dark, taller than a man. The leaves rasp together though the breeze is slight.

When his belly is full he wipes his hands on his trousers, takes a deep breath. Distant smoke tickles his nostrils. He ducks behind another tree, seeing now the whole garden: a scab of earth for cabbages, a lattice of bean canes. Beyond squats a low house. Then, without warning, the mess of fruit froths up in his gut so he falls to his knees, heaving, spasming like a cat. His eyes film over and he passes out.

His vision, when he focusses again, is washed with lemon-coloured light. The sun has risen into a sky like brass. A few feet from him a thrush smashes a snail against a stone, stabs with his beak at the desperate slime. He watches the bird swallow, its eye on him bright and dispassionate, before it flies away.

The shutters of the house have been opened. A woman stumps out onto the verandah and sets down a canary in its cage. The bird immediately begins to sing, thin coils of sound that seem to the listening man clear yellow like the creature itself.

He lies still, spying on the woman. She rocks into the garden on bad feet, bending stiffly to pick something off a geranium. She twitches her headscarf into place, tucks it beneath her chin. The man recalls his wife adjusting her own scarf that last morning, her hands quick and neat, smoothing her hair out of sight.

The crone closes her eyes, lifts her face to the sky. He wonders if she is praying. They pray differently, these others: alien gestures, an alien god. The dust of her ancestors and his sift together beneath the good black earth, the splintered bones of both lifted by the plough: it doesn't matter. She is not his kind. Her hands stay at her sides. He's glad, thinking he will have to squeeze the breath from her throat if she signals anything holy.

But perhaps he groans, or says his wife's name out loud, because the old women spots him, rounds on him swift as nightmare, lunging at him with a spade. He tries to stand but she shoves him hard in the chest and he sprawls, winded. She shouts at him, scolds him in her language, jabs him in the ribs. This makes him vomit again, but sour bile merely. He swears afterwards and is then quiet. She clams too, squinting at him, chewing the insides of her cheeks. He listens to the canary singing, watches ants troop past his fingers with the fragments of a maimed butterfly. On his bare face the sun burns like molten copper.

She grasps his hand, helps him stagger to his feet. She makes clucking noises, purses her lips as she yanks his head by the hair, turning his face this way and that. Finally she comes to a decision, beckons him to follow her up the steps to the verandah, thrusts him down onto a skinny chair too ornate for this house. Something stolen, he thinks, something looted.

He watches her go inside, fossicking in the shadows. Sunlight gilds a photo of a bearded man outside a farm-house. Little girls sit at his feet, their hair tightly braided, eyes solemn. It is this house, he realises. The woman passes into another room. He wonders if there is a phone, if she's calling some hulking son or brother. He observes bright flecks of dust spinning, falling. He feels empty, insubstantial, the husk of something.

He strokes the railing of the verandah, the wood slivered and scaling under his hand. A few days ago he was painting his own house, sanding the porch in long, smooth sweeps, like grooming a horse. Then the paint, forget-me-not blue. Eased from the can, the lid clattered away. He stirred the creamy paint with an old stick, dipping the brush carefully so the excess pleated back. His wife came with a jug of lemonade, tart and good, in a tumbler with roses round the rim, the only unbroken glass from the set his mother had given them. He tapped his wife on the nose with a paint-stained finger and she twirled away laughing, graceful despite the fullness of her belly, the weight of their long-awaited child.

The old woman returns with a tin tray. She is muttering, crossly it seems to him. She eases the blood-crusted shirt from his shoulders, probes the hold where the bullet passed through. She isn't gentle. As she leans close, snuffling out any stink of rot that might be thickening in his gut, he can see the white hairs on her chin, the pouched mouth. He can detect the solemn-eyed little girl, though in fact this crone appears neither male nor female to him. Scarcely human, in fact. More plant-like, a tuber of sturdy growth, invincible and slow. A weed that splits stone.

She makes him strip, orders him back down the steps to the garden. She lathers him with a block of green soap. He cries then, without shame, face and nose slimed with tears. She wipes him clean and he stands naked on the earth. She brings buckets, flings cold water over him till his sobbing stops and he gasps and shivers, all wet and glittering in the sun.

On his hip a boot-print is marbled purple beneath the skin. She smears this with foul-smelling slave, as she does his pulped cheek. She gives him trousers he has to cinch tightly with a belt. She dresses the ragged bullet wound. He says 'thank you' in her language – one of the few words he knows; that and 'hello, how's it going?'. She appears not to notice, makes him sit again, brings him black tea, sharp white cheese, signing to him as if he's stupid that he must eat slowly. She sits opposite, embroidering white cloth with red thread, some unfathomable design.

He dips the bread in his tea and chews with difficulty: a few teeth are broken, one is loose. Hauling himself into the lorry when he was rounded up he'd tried to hurry and slipped. He'd taken a rifle slammed into his face for that …

He'd thought the smallness of his village would protect them. The littleness of a place where you know everyone by sight; where neighbours nod even if they don't speak as you pass on the way to the two coffee-houses, one each side of the square. His wife had fussed like a chicken whenever the news was bad, but he told her: Your name means hope, woman. How is it that you have none? She gave him a cool look, her mouth tight, so that she seemed old to him, and he said: Hot words from firebrands in the cities. This'll burn itself out, you'll see.

They came when she was at her mother's and he was glad of that. A plain morning with the smell of paint in the air, the truck dark, snouted up his street like a beast. The men in its maw were bound, already anonymous, passive. The captors drove to the good fishing place by the river, kicked them, beat them. One or two had sticks. Then they stood around, smoking cigarettes, not talking, suddenly sheepish. The man lay in the brambles and watched the olive-coloured water sliding over the flat stones. A man came over, unzipped his flies, pissed on the grass near his face: it was the pharmacist, his clean, pink hands grazed now, raw.

At dusk the victors drove off, chatty as they boarded the lorry, shouting obscenities, laughing, the bright sparks of their cigarettes brief trails of light. The man felt giddy, light-headed with relief, ashamed at his elation as he staggered up. They worked at each other's bonds, limped down the lane swearing vengeance, arms round shoulders. The man was alone, though, as he turned to his own house, and he still thought it would come to this and no more. He thought: we'll have to break some windows, thwack some skulls. and when the sickness is out of us there will be quiet again for another generation.

The house was dark as he entered, but the television was on, barking questions from a quiz show. He smelled cigarettes. When he switched on the light he saw first the gloss of blood on her thighs, her white, wet skin where the skirt was ripped. Cigarette butts on the floor, and cigarette packets, different brands. His wife looked at him, her eyes dark with knowledge …

He winces as he eats. The old woman grunts, seizes his jaw, her hand meaty as a labourer's. She yanks out the incisor with a single clean jerk, throws it over the railing onto the soil, where it glistens like a plump seed. She laughs, leans over, spits on it. Says something that makes her laugh harder. And loses interest in him completely. She wheezes across to a table crowded with herbs, cuttings, scaly bulbs. He watches her veined hands snipping, pulling, patting the plants as in some ritual of practised grace. He sips the tea, the flavour of the black leaves and his own blood harsh in his mouth, like metal. He curls his tongue into the fresh cavity.

... That night he went to the pharmacists's house, some distance from the village, isolated. The pharmacist wasn't home, his wife told him. She opened the door with shy courtesy, her eyes widening when the light from the hallway fell on him. No, she didn't know when her husband would be back. It would be better to come back the next day. When he forced the door she only whimpered, seized her baby from its cradle. Both mother and infant smelled milky, made the same meowing noise. He stood in the kitchen, his fists clenching and unclenching at his sides. He wanted her to be quiet, so he could think. When he struck her the child thucked onto the tiles with a sound like a flour-bag splitting.

He waked until dawn, the sparkling swarf of stars above his head. They picked him up at first light, the lorry roaring down on him as he stood dumbly by the side of the road. They were driven for hours. Then they were shoved off the truck, blinking and stumbling, the same beaten men who'd sworn vengeance, the captors the same. The man looked for the pharmacist, but couldn't see him, though he recognised nearly everyone else. Their captors told them to dig, threw them spades, which were all stamped: municipal parks department. Those that didn't have spades were forced to dig with bare hands. He scooped the soil behind him like a dog, first on his knees, finally on his belly. The captors drank coke, bottles flashing amber as they tilted them back.

After sunset they were lined up along the lip of the pit. The light was violet, shredded with bats. There was the scent of rain edging in from the south, and the night-breath of trees,. He didn't hear the bullet, was only jolted into the grave, the air knocked from his lungs as someone thudded on top of him. He smelled turf; was reminded of weekend soccer games, the muddy pitch and the slide after the ball ...

The old woman is in the vegetable patch, singing among the cabbages. As he walks towards her she smiles at him, her mouth hung with spittle. His shadow falls on her like a stain. He kneels. She has gathered an apronful of plums, pops one into his mouth. He chews the rags of its flesh, the juice sour in his throat. He eases a cabbage from the earth. It creaks as it comes, the veined leaves damp on his hands. She nods and passes him a trowel, watches as he slides the blade into the earth, loosens another cabbage, cradles it in his lap. The core of the vegetable is heavy, like a man's head, and when he tears a leaf it rips with a snapping softness, the sound of the dead limbs under him as he clawed and climbed the heap of bodies, the corpses cooling under the stars.

The handle of the trowel is smooth in his grip, the sweated wood warm. He closes his eyes and listens to the canary, the glitter of its singing, and the old woman humming beside him. He feels the sun scorch the skin of his back, peeling him away, splitting him open like a plum.

Gavin Dunlop

Body on a Beach

Running, running with skirts raised
chorus lines of petticoat waves
cancan for shore

ending in the splits
and a wild united roar
into the face of land.

To the sound of taffeta
uncrushing, the waves release
a body beached.

Trailing hems of leaving foam
darken the sand like cast nets,
capturing a mock applause

of hands abandoned by the surf,
stirring them a little in its infinite
encores, but not enough;

drowned man, an audience of one
not clapping, like all death:
less well behaved than silence.

The Hopetoun House Tigers

Throned on an elephant`s chair-saddle rack
in plumed pith helmet and khakis,
parasolled from the sun`s ferocious attack
you bagged us.
                    Loading a camera
after emptying your gun, a punkawallah
snapped you proud with a boot on our backs
for your sepia hero-of-Bengal album.
You gave us Kiplingesque names for fun
and to tell us, later, one from one.

We kept our heads, you made rugs of our skins,
chucking the rest - the flesh of gold.
A taxidermist cored uninhabited skulls
replacing the brains with scaffolding,
untrained in what to do with souls.

Boat Trip to Staffa

A stone mushroom in a barren field
is a cold and lonely yield for all
that churning by the plough-Atlantic,

licked smooth by rough-tongued winds
that root among these bare degrees
through thistle sprays of sea
like rabid prowls of dog-storm.

Only sun`s beleaguered beams
give neighbourhood to existence;
rain prunes the look of land,
mist the growth of distance.

Arriving then at Fingal's cave,
thought saved for awe captures instead
wave-wielding winds, wild cold
and the raw omnipresence of time;
the labours of weather, not the sculptures
they render, rouse a sense of the sublime.

While grey seals and cormorants plunge
and resurface, repeatedly unamazed.

Meadow

I want to laze in the long green grass
down here.

I want to stare at the deep blue sky
up there.

I don`t want to hear the silvery scythe
come near.

The grass is too lush to be sheared
by fear.

Like a sunflower bending, heavy with bliss,
let me lay back
and yellow the green of the meadow

for years and years and years.

Lake Tahoe

Paddle-ships unzip water
bursting whites from blue,
together towed in spreading fans
then closing to blue, unopened ever.

Sierra slopes, stadium-tight
with wild shrub, pine and fir,
surround the field of blue;
greens, browns and pink-whites
whisper 'standing room only,
the view is sold out'.

The sky above made flesh by blue
kisses the water - in love,
never taking their eyes off each other.

For myself, tiny on the lip sand
of lake-shore, I stand explored
by the water`s licks and wonder
at the cosmic generosity of blue,
one huge colour by which all others
are so intimately found.

Walking in Woods

Of birds
I can empty trees with a footstep,
trigger a twig innocently,
kill a quiet sky.

Of words,
those shoes that thought wears
to travel and be heard by,
you can empty me with a teardrop
falling (it seems) accidentally,
fill me with terrified whys.

For your hurt`s
reason I listen, inert, hearing
only the blood of its silence
trickle dumbly and glisten

like the sap from a twig
that I broke in a wood
where I earlier thoughtlessly stepped.

Shona Dougall illustration to 'Walking in Woods'

On Lighting a Candle in a Cathedral

I light a candle in a cathedral
amid hushed stone, old air,
a ghost congregation of prayers.

I light it to douse one small darkness.

Neighbour candles dwell
on their own affairs,
each a stranger with a sadness.

My candle is there because a prayer
surprised me, unsure yet feeling right;
its eternal tongue, pale and strong,

languaging through silent flame
the believing part of doubt.

Footballer

Kickin a ba, kickin a ba
ah spent ma life jist kickin a ba
fae heid tae toe tae knee tae wa
an back again.

When ah wis young ah kicked it in the air
ah kicked it bluddy onywhere
nae control, nae cares
never ane tae keep it oan the grun.

Doin time, doin time
ah spent ma life jist doin time
fae dreams tae schemes tae bettin lines
an back again.

While pigeons an the ither lads were prancin
peckin dowts an practisin
fur goin tae the dancin
ah wis the tenement yuppy playin keepy-uppy.

Watchin ma life, watchin ma life
ah spent ma life jist watchin ma life
fae crib tae crime tae wummen tae wine
an back again.

Kickin a ba.
Missin a ba.
Kickin the bucket.
Snuffin it.

Child of the Glasgow Tenements

Anda Paterson

These ornately decorated high ceilings, long windows, drafts, dust, spiral staircase, brass-knobbed wooden balustrades with decorative iron spars, moss-covered steps to the old steamy – this was a 'wally close'. It was shattered during the War by bombs. Everything was slightly askew!

I always say I was born in the Botanic Gardens, my first memory being left in a pram in a warm atmosphere with long-leaved exotic plants swaying gently against the brilliant light of the arched tracery of the Kibble Palace, small birds, trapped, chittering in the background. We were tended by a pure white lady in marble. Indeed, many 'marbles' languished around while our mothers had tea and scones in the café at the entrance gate. We grew up in the Botanics. On wet days we ran into the glass houses to touch the colourful flowers, the orchids, the cacti, every plant you could imagine. We were making so much noise the long-suffering 'parkie man' evicted us into the rain. "This racket will frighten the flowers, and they will wither and die."

We tiptoed out ashamed. At least the girls did. We could not allow the flowers to die. But the boys stamped their feet and howled. The flowers did not die. On good days the sun shone. The park benches were packed with people squashed together – monumental figures, with prams, newspapers, walking sticks and ice-cream cones. When one person left, another took their place. A child was not allowed to take up a place. All kinds of people crammed together in long rows, facing the sun. I remember the long rows, the stillness of the sitting figures: they would be there forever. We children were not allowed to sit on the grass or pick daisies.

We lived near the BBC. All nationalities lived nearby. This area was the 'digs' for the BBC, Scottish National Orchestra and the theatres. Upstairs was a Russian lady whose house was full of icons. Gold and silver enthroned madonnas with child glowed in the candlelight. Another family collected Japanese saints in black-lacquered frames. We lived next door to Fergusson and Margaret Morris who reputedly lived on porridge and vegetables! My grandfather took me to the Art Gallery every weekend: he worshipped at the painterly Rembrandts, I went to the Madonnas, the school of Botticelli, Giorgione and the Bellinis. These were my 'pals'.

My Scottish grandfather took me walks in Bute. He told long stories of history, of Scott, of Burns. My English grandmother did *not* approve. (A military family, they were punctual, disciplined and stoic. "No dreadful poetry from that awful man – filling a child's head – in this house!")

There were exhibitions of Van Gogh and Gaugin in Kelvingrove. Everyone went. When one left the galleries all people appeared to be like a Van Gogh or a Gaugin. This powerful metamorphosis went on for days. My grandfather was a signwriter, frequently completing gilded lettering on site: *Gentlemen, Ladies, Exit, Stairs* etc, while the Scottish Orchestra rehearsed. I tagged along. The seated figures with musical instruments, on flimsy chairs (the instruments and men being one) were fascinating – how to make a symphony work, a piano concerto sing.

We were evacuated during the war to Darvel – a town child exposed to country life – black and white designed Ayrshire cows, great Clydesdale horses with feathered feet filled one's imagination. What bliss!

But it was not all bliss. There was primary school, a sea of tumbling 5-year-olds, 47 of us crammed into a dank classroom, with slates and squeaky white pencils which shattered when they hit the floor. I asked permission to go to the loo. Having no sense of direction, I ended up in the 'boys'. There were lots of little furry animals with great whiskers and long tails, scooting up and down the leaky pipes. So I fed them during my 'elevenses'. They became tame. I repeated this for some days, but was at last found out! My mother was called: I was supposed to know the difference between hamsters and rats aged 5½ years. No one had told me.

This proved a blessing. Diptheria ensued, followed by TB. There was no vaccination, and God be praised no school! I drew and drew, wrote rhyming words (badly spelt) looked at picture books and was read to frequently. I was not particularly ill with either illness, the only trouble that I might get better too quickly and have to return to school!

Summers were spent in Bute – the sea, rock pools, mountains, hill walks, monsters in the sea (porpoises in early summer) and building houses under the flowering rhododendron bushes. We went by paddle steamer 'doon the watter', passing landscape after landscape often shrouded in rain, and the white sparkling slipstream behind the steamer.

And there the High School of Glasgow for Girls. Glasgow School of Art followed, and then my first teaching post at Garnethill School. I wore out the pavements of Garnethill relentlessly, every crack and cranny familiar. Did I like school? I loved art, music, science and geography but slept through the rest. I did like my teachers who were patient and kind, tolerating my endless drawing during their subjects. I remember many of them being socialist – strongly so, to the chagrin of my grandmother. I wanted to 'do' life drawing but it was still life – the dreaded 'still life'!

At art school you could draw what you wanted. Large compositions of my grandparents and great aunts, the old soldiers from the model lodging houses sitting on the gravestones near Templeton's Factory, the vendors of the Saltmarket, the winos and down-and-outs of London, Paris and Glasgow, the beggars and gypsies of Andalusia and the Algarve. Why 'do' the down-and-outs and gypsies? For a start they sit still and do not mind if you draw them. They are already preoccupied. At GSA I was sympathetically encouraged by William and Mary Armour, David Donaldson, Benno Schotz, my extra subject being stained glass with Walter Pritchard. I loved lines around everything!

One of the purposes of art is said to release the viewer from the restraints of life and give pleasure, escape and appreciation of beauty. I do not fulfil this in any sense. The messy untidiness of human life and the ridiculous, absurd and comic on the other hand, struggling, anxious and sometimes tragic. This is my subject matter.

No romantic dreaming or glamour, but the human figure before being 'tidied up', polished and romanticised, at that moment before people are aware of being observed. I am particularly fascinated by the structure and formation of the human head and hands, trying to use the creases, hollows, baggy skin, folds around the knuckles and wrists. It is amazing the expressiveness at the emotional level, how much is revealed about an individual by the movement of hands. I use any excuse to observe hands and faces and then to emphasise, and enlarge, heads and gnarled hands.

With irony and poetic justice I am rapidly developing a strong resemblance to my own paintings of confused humanity, having chased and stalked, recorded many images of *un*exceptional people. We are deeply influenced by our early experiences and environment and cannot escape our childhood impressions having a profound imprint upon us. I draw and paint what I observe and know of their life and mind, with I hope some sympathetic observation – the sacred monumental human being.

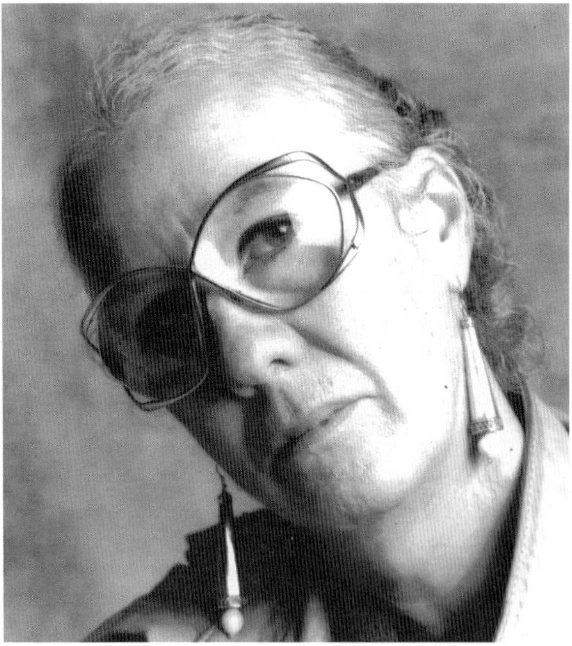

Anda Paterson

Anda Paterson

Whistling Goat Herder

The Quiet Woman

Street Musicians, Glasgow

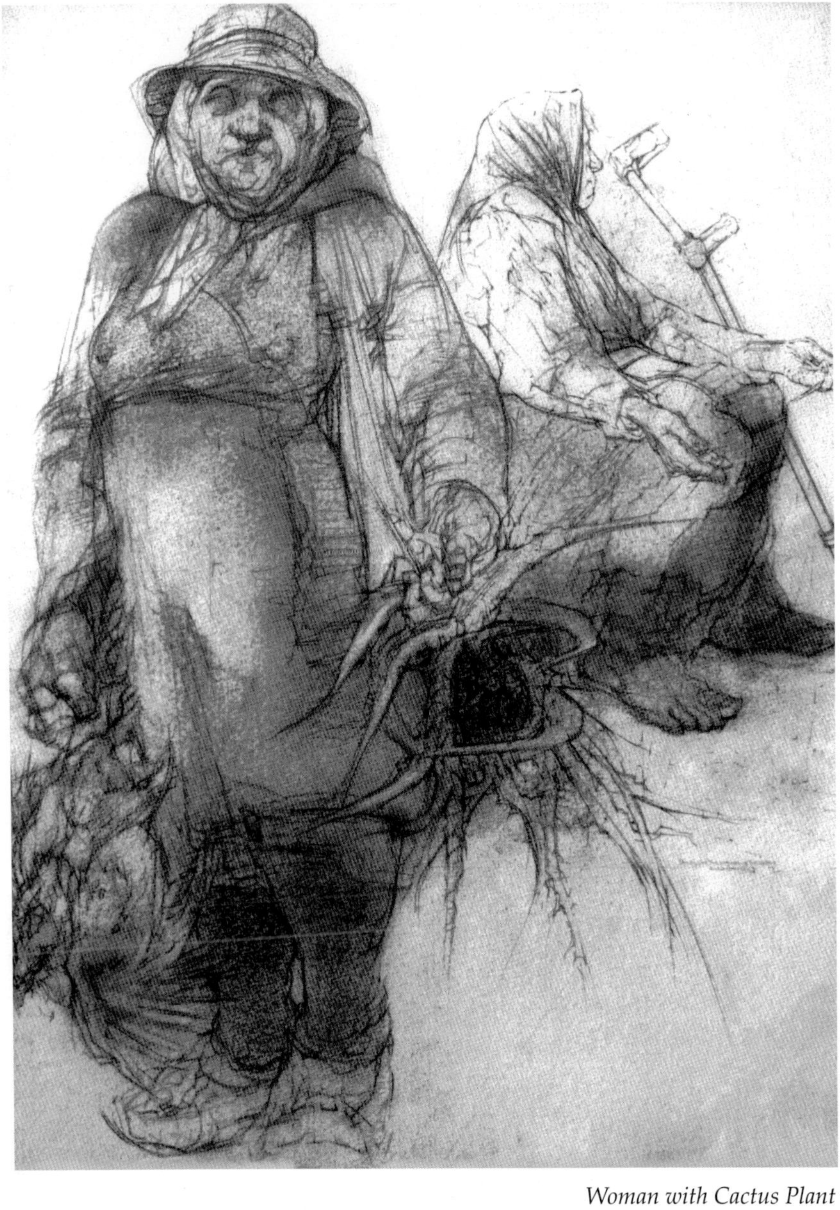

Woman with Cactus Plant

The Fisherman's Cats

The Bicycle Man, Saltmarket

The Beggar's Feast

Gossips, Rocha de Pena

Gypsy Family

Charity of the Gypsy

Golden Oxen

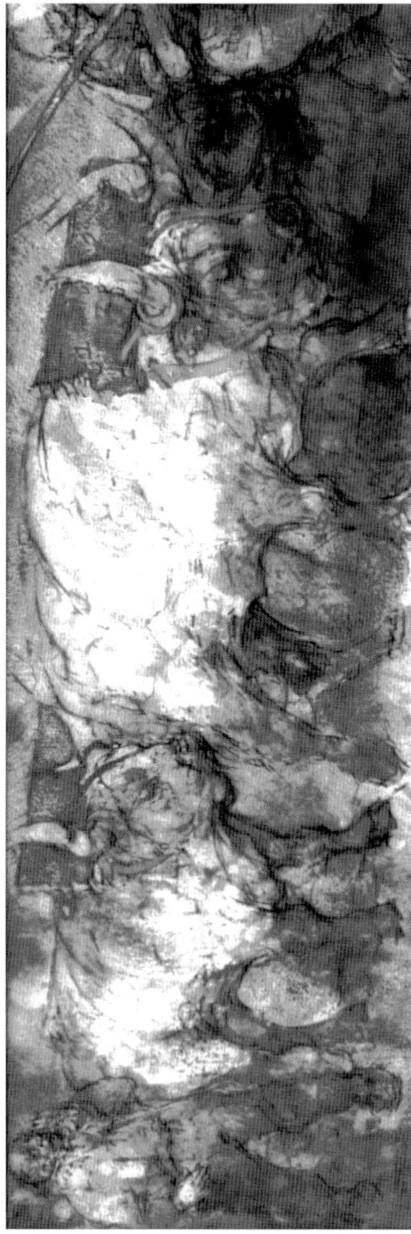

Women of the Dovecote

Donald Mackay

To Europa

In the field overlooking the shore
the bull is uneasy,
the long, deep wave of his roar
follows us down into the waves

steady and deep the lengths of his horn
calling and calling
waning and waxing, the bodily groan
growing on us two walking

into the water, unsteadily pursued
across the sand.
If, as we fear, the massive Simmental should
burst his fence and

with all a bull's dark terror
take to our heels
and foam after us into the foam; my daughter
and I would be way out of our depth.

If he followed us
both shore and sea lie entirely naked
to Europe,
and we have walked right into it
up to our necks. Watched slyly by Jupiter.

The Dynamo

We stayed overnight with him, who
for his power, rolled his own
out of a burn below the house.
I sensed that it should be different;
a different electricity, maybe
running silver out of the bulbs.
In his impossible house
he presided like Prospero
while we sat, waiting for wonders.

But anybody can, he explained.
Think of a bicycle dynamo,
its buzz as you pedal on the flat;
then the great roar in your ear

as you tip down
faster over the hill like water,
your light before you like a bow spray,
the black road appearing and appearing
as if you had invented it.

That night we turned on the lights
as if they were taps.
They shimmered a little
like the light off a water
he had drawn from his own source.
And when he switched them off
it was so very dark;
the whole house was filled
with the darkness of running water.

Jenny Long-Legs

I had a toy like this one once, its spindle-shanks
rising into the air with all the speed
a rubber band could muster. Yet she rises.
Also that un-necessarily elongated body
always dragging her back into the ground.
Yet she is mistress

over this contraption of needle and thread.
Just watch. Late August five o'clock sunlight
it is utterly windless,
perfect weather for a maiden flight.
You can hear her getting all revved
winding her band down in the grass

then she ups
so slowly. It is the early days of flight
my will is going with her higher
getting out of sight, and shouting, 'Bleriot!
Bleriot!' She must be up among the treetops
now. I think I can just about see her

late sun gleaming on her wings
dope-and-paper things. And I would be
a jenny, for the smallness of her
so wobbly,
all tiny struts and strings
as the day swiftly swallows her.

And she is air.

Before the Photograph

When, before the taking of photographs,
he and she started this
opening of one other button by button,
the desire in their hands
simply to be where they did not yet belong

but having so far no maps or graven images
of *terra incognita;*
they found what I found this morning,
a surprise passage
that I had never noticed, a path leading to water

the rank grasses that parted before my hands,
with a yearning
to leave the road, go down to the water.
And so it was I knew,
never having seen it before,
that I was not wrong to go that way.

And so he, with his first fingers
opening buttons
shirt and skirt buttons, he would have found her
just as open and fresh, and as rank
as he parted the grasses, all the way down to Eve.

Taiga

I have begun dreaming of trees again,
having seen them come back almost suddenly.
For I returned twenty years ago,
so to speak, over the weekend.
Where I found barrens,
as I had thought, gone under-cover,
gone

like a dream that follows on
its own well-hammered way;
then curves behind a tree, and vanishes.
Instead, there were thickets of briars,
birch-stands, sallow and alder bushes.

And openings, soft grooves
and hollows down a twisting path of grass,
with blaeberries, purple jewels, dripping
hidden either side;

with dappled hands, parting
screen after screen of green shade.
Then slipping
like grace

out into sunlight. So I have begun to see
no longer little woods, but forests
where you may set out in spring;
and meet no roads by autumn.
And pass, as in a dream
under the sun and moon, under the trees.

Until the sea.

Sula Bassana

(for George Legg)

If we had been looking South, they would have been
long arms of the wind-farm
down by the Causwaymire. But we were East
walking the eastern coast.
As, like the blades of a turbine
they revolved, they resolved into the form
of great birds, suddenly appeared
as if for us, over the horizon.

Turning like planetary time, the hours
the wings as wide as oars.
That finned, narrowed; dropped and speared,
disappeared among the shoals of herring.

Then up and out, turning again. I know
it was the fish that they were after,
having their reasons and their purposes
and not for us.
But there they were, revolving like an orrery
and then they went.

I never saw them go
the sky went blank
suddenly. As if a vision of the spheres
had gone; leaving an arc
for the universe, a mark
on the retina for truth;
as the earth sank away into sky,
rolling away from us.

The First Season

W D Fyfe

Sometimes in the twilight of a big summer night, I can still taste the smell of Africa. So I sit on my balcony and watch faint stars over the bold city lights until I fall asleep in my chair. Photographers say that once you've touched Africa, you can never leave it again. They say it's like the haunt of an old tune that you can't quite remember. I remember it clearly. It's the low deep song mothers hummed to their children in the back bush. It has a lullaby sound and a steep darkness. I can see it. It has gathered its babies and sits in the light of an open fire whose golden tongues lick their faces. Its children are quiet, their sleepy eyes tucked into the heart-smooth tempo of their mother's body. It feels warm and soft and close. And there, just in the shadows, is Norman Moon, his broad green back holding the dancing fire off the older children's faces, his crumbling granite voice keeping their eyes motionless. He is a murderous Scheherazade and tonight, like every night, he's telling the children stories.

When I knew Norman Moon, he was already old. He liked sweet tea, fat socks and smoked filthy French cigarettes. And he liked me, I think because soldiering is boring and I was the only real change in that first Zambezi summer. Terrible men with nothing to do cling to small excitements and cherish them. So, for one whole hot summer, my job was to listen to the brag and make the so-often stories new again: three months and one day of lying around in the heat, walking the bush, guarding a four goat village and a dust crossroads, with the same men I saw yesterday and the same ones I'd see tomorrow. In the beginning, he would casually find me and drop bits of advice into our conversation, slowly showing me how to live along the broad plain of the Zambezi River. I was young and wise and thought he was an old fool but I did keep my hair short, inspected my toes for fungus and never told him to clear off. Then, as the monotonous hot moved on and the others lost their love for a new listener, he just assumed me, as his. I found out he was from Glasgow and had started out, 'as a wee lad, mind', fighting for King and country on the wicked retreat out of Burma during World War II. He'd stayed with it, fighting the colonial wars until both he and Britain were too damned tired to care anymore. But when he went back to Scotland, he was just in time to witness his home dying on the unemployed Clyde.

"I couldn't stay, Cuddy," he said, "Terrible place. Cold and dirty. Aye. Used up like. Not one man in twenty workin. Pitchin pennies and sellin postcards and no jam for your bread. It's a great shame. No, Cuddy: the works are stopped and they'll no start again. And nobody gives a fiddler's fart for the lot of it."

He had a sister who wrote to him – once a month, without fail. He told me she handled all his money. She sent him his socks and her letters were full of lively stories about his nieces, the relatives and her husband. He never read his letters to me, but in the breathless afternoons, he would recall for himself these visits until I got to know the family. His nieces were exceptional students, gifted in the arts, musical and athletic. They would certainly marry well. His brother-in-law, despite a slow start, had gone on to find a good job in the clothing profession, but it was his sister, 'Our May,' who was the smart one and always had been.

"It's good to hear, Cuddy. Home like. People you remember, 'specially here at the dark end of the fuckin earth," he said once.

"Do you ever think about going back?"

"No, there's nothin for it. I tried. Plumber's helper, me. Fifty years old and carryin the tack for a wee lad out from the trade school. Then down to the pub and home to your bed. Every day! Aye, and up to your eyes in muck and shite an aw. And, it wis other people's! Whaur's the joy in that? So I says, 'Norman, get off your arse. Soldierin's whit ye ken. Go on back tae Africa and find ye a nice warm war'."

Nearly every evening, when the dark African night fell on us, he would walk down the path to the village – carelessly – as if he was out for a stroll. He would greet the adults there, and in a surprise, rediscover the children who were waiting in the same place, by the fire, just close enough to give him room to sit. And there in the strange light, among the night sounds of Africa, Norman Moon would tell the children stories. They were a bit muddled by his memory and the difficulty of language, but still quite distinctly the Scottish folk tales of his own childhood. He spoke them out slowly in Shona, the singing language of the Rhodesian bush, and Scots or English when there were no African words. The children, held by his magic voice, never moved. To them there was nothing strange about a tough worn white man coming to see them every night. They took it on faith, all of it, trusting the teller as much as the tale. And every night it was the same: Norman's gritty voice tracing over the lullaby mother sounds that had been singing to the babies of Africa for centuries. Then, as the songs began to die away, the children fading their eyes, their heads nodding, Norman would falter and yawn or stretch. It was time for bed. It was time for the mothers to gather them up and sleepy, slip them away safely into the darkness. Then Norman would sit and blow smoke with the men for long moments and talk politics and crops, the way men do in every corner of the world when the women are gone.

Just before the weather turned, about half of our company, including Moon, flew out to Salisbury on leave. I watched him disappear south in the helicopter and spent a week sitting in the shade with a Spaniard named Mendez and a coughing forgotten Irishman. I was sick of warm Coca Cola and stupid patrols in the blank bush.

"Don't be in such a hurry, Cuddy," they said. By then they all used

Moon's name for me. "As soon as the heat's over, the floppies will come."

Then, on one still afternoon indistinguishable from all the rest, the heat broke, high in the north and the rain came straight off the horizon in a maniac storm that thundered and cracked through my chest and left me cold and shivering. We sat smoking and talking in the afternoon darkness, head down, like dumb animals, our voices shouting into the pounding sound of the rain.

"Tomorrow," Beatty said.

"Two days," Mendez answered, "When it's dry. Then, Cuddy, we'll find you some war."

"Moon?" I asked.

"They'll be back in the morning and then we'll move out."

"Who's staying here?" I asked, worried that it might be me.

"Nobody. Nobody guards this village; it's too poor for the terrs

"Then why the fuck have we been sitting here all summer?"

"Moon likes it here." It was such a statement of fact that I swallowed any other protest I had about wasting three months of my life.

In the morning, the helicopters came back – with Moon and the rest of the men and possibly every bottle of beer available in Salisbury. That night we sat together and drank. The way men do when they need to swagger and bolt down their fears. The night was cool and wet, so we sat close to the fire and savaged the beer and each other.

"I'm tellin ye it'd work. 12 men, 15 then, and ye could …"

"Fuck you, English! Best, best, best! Fuck you!"

"Anyway, the truck's into it up to the hubs and nobody laughin but …"

"Oh Jesus! Tell us about the Legion. Sure as fuck we haven't heard enough about the Legion."

Shouts and shards thrown into the night, unheard and unheeded, like some local sports club gathered at the pub to work out the schedule, their accumulating energy spilling over into a shrill beer binge.

"Three girls! Beautiful, just beautiful, like little black flowers."

"No idea, but I do know …"

"Now the women in Mombasa! There you go …"

"So I rolled over the edge and …"

And that's the way it went, into the night – a drunken free-for-all that spared no one – anger and laughing and disagreements bubbling up with the beer and washing away just as quickly.

"Cuddy's looking for a war. Thinks he's …"

"Jan? Who's the Dutchman, son of a bitch, ye remember? He was wi …"

Fantastic, elaborate plans – for victory, ammo belts, a goat farm in retirement, some extraordinary woman. Tough, cold men who could only show friendship, taunts and teases: so drunk any slander was acceptable.

"The kaffir can't fight – it's a known fact. He just doesn't have …"

"Is that what they teach at the university? You a communist, Cuddy?"

"I'm just saying ..." No one and nothing was sacred, except Norman Moon who sat and drank and listened. He was exempt.

Then, as the night waned on and we each started hoarding our private stash of beer, there were silences and less mischief. And a few quiet sticks poking at the fire. And to fill up the quiet, the stories began – old stories, but ones I hadn't heard before, told in earnest, by men who weren't joking anymore. Names I'd never heard, places they'd never talked about. Stories about Katanga and the Sudan and Nigeria, stories about killing and desperate attempts to stay alive. Stories about men whose only purpose on earth was to slaughter other men, as quickly and as efficiently as muscle and technology would allow. And in the background, in the darkness, from the village, we could hear mother Africa, singing to her babies, hugging them close against the black night and the horrible fire up on the hill, where foreign warriors were sharpening their weapons.

Late the next morning, we packed our gear away in the helicopters and turned north, for the Zambezi. We stalked a waterhole and waited. For two days and two nights we watched the antelope drink and a pride of lions that was watching them. Then, on the third day, the lions moved off and Moon told us to go to sleep that night. In the morning, a group of guerrillas came padding out of the bush. There were a dozen of them, talking and joking on their way to war. We ambushed them perfectly and killed five – four in the firefight, and one more after they surrendered.

"Dinnae come here!" Moon shouted at the prisoners lined up in front of him, "I'll kill ye. I'll kill yese aw. Awa hame – there!" He pointed north, to the river.

He turned slightly and shot the man closest to him. It was at such close range that the force of the slugs tore away most of his chest, even before they knocked him into the air. Then he fell and bounced in the dirt. Yet he was still alive, and he lay there, gurgling and twisting for breath.

"Get oot o here," Moon said, low and matter-of-factly. "Awa hame!"

The man on the ground wheezed and squirmed, his torn lung flapping like a rag trying to mop up the crimson bubbles that foamed out of him every time he sucked a breath. He arched his back in a frantic stutter for air. Then he died, and all that was left was a thick sticky red ooze in the dirt – and we all watched. Moon looked at the prisoners again and pointed north. Then we turned our backs and walked away. It was over before anybody knew it was happening and we never looked back.

That's what we did: stalked and killed, until we were swollen with blood and all the faces and all the places ran together. It became a routine, like delivering milk: the intensity of war swallowed by its own smooth, regular features. It only changed once that whole season.

We watched the families moving in a line through the bush, so we left the trap open. When they were clear of the scrub, three of us stood up and shouted. Their men opened fire and then ran, leaving the women and children. On the flank, we killed seven, before they got away. Moon walked forward and grabbed one of the dead men by the leg and dragged him bouncing, back to where the women were.

"Is this whit ye want?" He swung the dead man through the dirt.

"Dae ye no love your babies?"

The corpse landed with a dull thump.

"Look at it!" Moon shouted, "I'll have your children, ya evil things, and by Christ I'll chop 'em into stewin for my tea."

"Now tak yersel hame – there!" He pointed over their heads, "There!"

Even we didn't move.

"You!" Moon shouted at one of the women. She shrieked and buried her face in her hands. He grabbed one of her hands, and she howled.

"See this!" He pulled her, by the arm, to the dead man.

"Whaur are yer bairns?" The woman clawed at the dirt, screaming hysterically. In a tangle of arms and legs, she scrambled away, her bright cotton skirt billowing in the swirling dust. Two children ran to her and she pulled them down, desperately, trying to cover them with her body. She clung to them and stretched one arm out behind her towards Moon, as if that would stop him. He waited. In the long minutes, her frantic cries became a steady wail.

There are no ghosts in my dreams, just the quiet sounds of women singing, low and away in the far distance. So I must conjure them when I can, on quiet summer nights. Sometimes in the morning, when the city is still asleep, I wake up in the fading shallow darkness. I hear its steady breathing and feel the rhythms of its heartbeat. And as I watch the hollow yellow lights wink out like fallen morning stars, I wonder if the city knows what men are awake in its midst.

Anda Paterson, Shrove Tuesday *(continued from page 69)*

Richard Price

The Giant

Your first written message – a postcard, the Giant,
the rude Rude Man of quaint Cerne Abbas –
a long weekend with your parents –
cream teas, a cramped tea-room –
chairs that scrape the tiles.
"Where's his shorts?" your mother's chuckling,
"I knew friends got diseases from Thames-side jaunts."
Sometimes you can't see the light in people's eyes
but you know the light.

*

Your first
written message,

cheeky, cheerful,
cherished here –

"You risk …
Englishness."

I take
all the claptrap back,

the state identity
me me me,

I scrap the abstract,
the years

neck-deep in
neck-deep in.

I take almost all
the claptrap back.

*

Your note a taper, you'd started
to burn me clean –

amorous candlelight
and real marks of combustion

in this distant here,
this fifteen years here,
this two-lives-started-,
late-, later here.

Not a gift, a gift-tag.
Our old life the present.

*

Sometimes you can't see the light in a person's eyes
but you know the light.

*

No-one should act
as if love was resistance to enthusiasm,
one thing, one thing, one thing –
one thing, one thing –
as if love was agreeing
to reasonable expectations,
acceptance of a single species of love,
affection in monoculture,
passionate kisses for the coat-hanger, the word "love".

*

Forgiveness
tries to free us,
brings us close.

*

No-one thinks love
is Cerne Abbas as a naturist,
love as Cerne Abbas and Cerne Abbas as satire
(it's now thought Cerne Abbas was a satire –
on Cromwell) –

Thug-King God-Cromwell
slaughtering your Irish ancestors,
Club-Prick Bomber-Cromwell
slaughtering my English ancestors.

Love can't be,
truthfully, this prosey poetry.

Love can't be
the word "slaughtering",
centuries-long, repeated to a faction.

*

A chirpy postcard ("The First English Nudist") –

count a year or ten, a snoring evening, hand-in-weary-hand –
we're collapsed before the fireplace (blocked off).

The children are content around us, absorbed,
pretending to write.
Sometimes you can see, sometimes you can see
the light in a person's eyes – and you don't know the light.

*

Final goodbyes, all the risks and anxieties of a life,
dogs unmuzzled, owls on the last oak –
suited street sellers hawking the smallest kite in the world.

Please refile this lifetime's ladlit – leave the script
at the dentist's, with Practical Yachting,
Macho and Goodbye!

No time now for share and share alike,
madrigals in the zesty juice-bar, coughs, viscous waves,
Orchestre Baobab, nailed down windows
a claw-hammer cannot release.

And no hope of seeing you, more than a sister,
without hurt.

Final goodbyes, all the risks and anxieties of love.
No hope now (all the no's, all the now's)
for a better misunderstanding,
the thousand species once supported by a single oak,
a world created by a bright tattoo on a giant's back.

You see the light in someone's eyes
and you know that light.

Dense Hours

Music to sleep.

Do you still listen to discussions?
A paper-yellow light and you're fine-tuning,
a child again with pocket torch,
secret vitamins (raisins), a sponsored read.

Darkness can be held with a wedge of radio.
Darkness can dissolve if you can dissolve
in art appreciation, civil debate.

Will you remember, last night was it,
"The Need for Faith" made you, finally,
thankfully, neither here nor there?

I almost pray for us to sleep corrected, to breathe
synchronised, complementary breaths,
miles peacefully apart.

Music to sleep. No, the song's over and I
still can't lie still. When will the flat-out flickers
call the dense hours a day,
click themselves, me, gently off?

Music.

Her Planet

She lends me erotic records –
I know she's not leading me on.
I started the lending library,
books and poems, off and on.

I've loved her since
I became convinced
of the planet I was living on,
her planet.

Sharing a song is intimate,
it's hearing singing in the shower.
It's voice and face and touch,
it's lips and poise and power.

I hear her songs
and sing along.
I sing badly, but I bless the hour,
I bless this planet.

She's half reluctant,
I hope she's not being kind.
She knows I'm trouble,
trouble I can't leave behind.

I'm afraid
some fine day
she'll leave me behind,
this silent blue planet.

A Patron for a Painter

Zerrin Otgur

Gustave Guyon, a peasant Frenchman surprised his farmer mother and father (and the fifty other labourers in his village) aged five when he asked for a brush, some paint – and an easel. He amazed them all again aged eighteen when he won on the basis of a single painting a full scholarship to Amsterdam's famed Academy of Art.

"We rarely see such creative vision, such truth – and in one so young!" the university board wrote to him. "Welcome to the Academy!"

Three years later, in the fall, Gustave Guyon graduated with distinction – to his mother and father's (and the fifty other villagers') delight. But Gustave himself saw graduation as a disaster.

The Academy proclaimed success all round but the 'success' seemed all on the university's side: it had squashed and stretched, boxed and stamped and spat out another of its patent wonders: a graduate. But the winner of the happy diploma, was by this act no longer a protégé but a member of the unemployed. He saw the university's victory as his own personal failure. He couldn't help it. With a mockery of a ceremony and a useless slip of paper, he was shunted out into an unfamiliar world.

The morning after the Academy officially washed its hands of him he bobbed back up outside the office of the Professor of Oils. He knew the old man well, loved him like a father. The professor answered his urgent knock, thinking it was a freshman. He was surprised to see Gustave.

"Didn't you just graduate?"

Gustave admitted that he had – unfortunately!

The professor sat his pupil down. "Why are you so afraid to leave this place?" he asked him gently.

I need your lectures and tutorials. They guide and instruct me."

"My tasks and these classrooms are a pale substitute for the world outside – a world we now give you leave to join. Go and find your path!"

Gustave sat where he was, looking even glummer. "I've no time to find a path. Without your regular assignments I'll run mad long before I do."

"It may *feel* as if you're going mad – at first, but you'll soon adjust."

He reached for the door, but Gustave grabbed his hand and said, "I was speaking literally."

"What do you mean?"

"I dream when I paint."

"All painters do."

"But most also dream in their sleep."

"REM is necessary," the professor agreed. "It's our time for making sense."

"I don't dream in my sleep."

"Impossible! You'd be a walking wreck – you'd be insane!"

"I didn't say I didn't dream. I do dream. "I dream while I create. So what will happen to me if I can't find any work?"

The professor saw that Gustave was sincere. He thought for a while. "I advise you to paint for yourself."

Gustave smiled. "I've tried, believe me, I've tried. My curse goes deeper than that: nothing comes to my brush without being called for."

"Please tell me I haven't spawned a hack!" said the professor in alarm. "Tell me you don't only bring out your brush for money!"

"I meant only that to do my art I must first believe it's needed."

"But now, just to survive, you'll have to take any job, whatever it is – as soon as it comes up! It's the very definition of a hack!"

"I'll go crazy before I become a hack!" young Gustave declared, but he saw the old professor could do no more for him, and left.

It was noon and he hurried down the steps into the tide of life. He had the idea of staving off lunacy by snatching a daydream or two chalking up the pavement with requests from passers by. He turned up the old Calves Street, the route the cattle once took to market, making for Dam Square, the free-for-all space in the heart of the city.

But that day the expanse of ancient cobblestones had a canvas wall round it and a guard at the gate. There was a blue-and-white banner on the side of a ticket booth. "The greatest show on earth!" it read. Through the gate Gustave saw a fun fair in full swing – people milling about the rides and gambling tents. Their shouts and squeals floated out to him. Popcorn scattered at his feet. He wanted to go in, but had no money.

He went up to a tubby, sad-faced man in a white suit and tie standing by the ticket booth, counting ticket stubs. "What show is this?" he asked.

Marten Breuker, the proprietor, turned to view the inquirer: a bearded man, pinched in a black mourner's jacket, and standing two inches out of his second hand trousers. He was plainly poor, clearly worthless, but the wonder in his face – it intrigued him.

"This is the World Amusement Park."

"You run this World?" the artist asked.

"I own it," said the businessman.

Gustave stood staring up over the wall at the looming Ferris wheel. It began to turn. He was a country boy, sick of nature's marvels, and he had never seen a more fantastic sight. "How beautiful!" he gasped.

Marten turned to his World searching for the grace the artist saw. The pride he felt when he looked at it in terms of money disappeared. He felt nothing but confusion, saw only senseless whirling things, mindless flashing things, heard only the honk and whine of a show so vulgar it was only tolerated in any city for a month at a time.

"What's so beautiful?" Marten asked, perplexed.

"I'm no good with words. I see in paint."

"You're an artist?"

"I'm a qualified painter."

The businessman stepped back coldly rom the artist. "My World is no place for an artist."

"Give me a place in it," Gustave insisted.

He tried to ignore it, but a craving filled the businessman of 59 long years to see something more than banknotes in his World, to see some of this charm he was a stranger to. "Can you paint its beauty for me?"

"It's all I can do."

Marten ordered a booth rigged up inside with a good view of the main attractions. He stocked it under the painter's instruction with an easel, a canvas, brushes, paint, rags, and turpentine. When all was ready, Gustave stepped in. "Commission me, then I can begin to paint."

"The beauty?"

"It's all beautiful."

Toward evening Marten squeezed into the artist's booth. He kicked over the turpentine. "Bit cramped in here," he added, by way of apology.

"Is it? What man thinks about the size of his bed while he is dreaming?"

"Quite so." Marten saw the change in Gustave's face: the gaunt freak was gone and a sane young man stood smiling at him, as if just waking from a restful sleep.

As the painter dabbed and smeared Marten stole a look over his shoulder at the work in progress. At first it made no sense to him, but then he saw. The World, his burden, his spouse, had shed its mask, one he had believed to be its face – a mask of tedium, of greed and empty arrogance. For the first time he glimpsed something of worth behind. His heart expanded. He stepped closer to this other World, held out his hand to it.

"It – it's magnificent!"

He forgot he was on the way to his compulsive hourly check of the fair's ticket sales. He dragged in a beer-crate seat and made his post by the painter's side. Gratefully he watched the roaring booming chaotic muddle of his World swept into meaning. Gustave left no side unexplored, and every time Marten thought him done he would start out again from a new angle to catch some new truth.

"Not happy with it yet?"

"Who can be happy with only one dream?"

"How do you see all this?"

"I look."

Marten did little else for the fair's whole stay but sit in the cubicle gazing at his World through the painter's eyes. He was not impatient for a finished work of art. He was on the painter's side, creation's side; happy to see old scenes go out, happy to see what new scenes came in. For the first time in his life he was a cheerful and contented man.

But the last week came, then the last day. Marten admired the steady way Gustave kept plying his brush despite the falling curtain, but when night came and there was still no wrapping up, no signing off, he knew that Gustave must be unaware of the date and time, of what it meant, that it meant the end. Marten did not want to tell him, had to, but didn't know how to, and the task hung over him spoiling the last few hours. Only with the fair turned off, taken apart, and being packed away, did he broach the subject with the artist who was – still painting.

"Time's up," he said, and put his hand over the painter's brush.

"Huh?"

"That's all I can ask from you."

"I was just getting started!"

"The World must move on."

Gustave was stunned. Where had all the time gone? There was so much time before. Would he have to give up his brush and quit the World unfinished? He stared at his painting, an abandoned work in progress, a Pompeii cut-off.

Marten picked up the canvas. He thought if he could own it he might keep his newfound love for his World alive, even once the artist himself was gone. I'll buy it," he declared.

"It's not ready."

"I think it is."

"I won't sell it."

"I'll give you whatever you want."

"I'm not a hack!" Gustave said, indignantly.

Marten felt hollow and confused as he oversaw Gustave pack up his borrowed paints, pull on his dreadful black jacket, and vacate his lodging in the World. Outside he stood with him awkwardly among the crates and cables. He was due at the freight office but he did not set off. He begged Gustave, who seemed in spirit to have left already, to sit with him awhile. On the dank bare boards of the merry-go-round he drank a flat beer with him, plied him with left-over popcorn. He recalled their first, their fateful, meeting, but trailed off without conclusion. Then suddenly he wished himself gone, away from this dead association, away from its awful wake, said a curt good-bye, and hurried off.

As Marten and the World without the artist clicked, whirred and honked through an early winter in Berlin he regretted every moment of that final scene. There was something he meant to say and should have said. If only he could only hold of the artist once more, his rose-coloured glasses, he would give him a permanent place in his World. His regret dragged him down and after Warsaw he could not go on to Vienna. For the first pale month of spring he and his World were back in Amsterdam.

He had barely stepped off the EuroCity train before he found himself, timidly climbing the ornate steps of the Academy of Art; heard himself humbly asking a lowly professor – an old man head to toe in oils and reeking of turpentine – for just one word of Gustave Guyon.

"You didn't hear?"

"Tell me!"

"Gustave graduated!"

Marten trudged back to Dam Square. The World was waiting for him there in freight cars ready to be unloaded. He gazed at it grimly. He considered giving it up altogether but the lingering hope that he might one day be able to see its charm again made him cling to it. Spiritlessly he oversaw it taken out of storage and set up.

One of Marten's many idle hands who helped erect the horror houses and death rides, had also put up Gustave's old booth. The lad used to set the painter's easel up, the paints and brushes too, even the beer-crate seat. But the booth was empty; and this disturbed Marten deeply – he couldn't say why. He searched out the boy and bellowed at him. But when the boy offered to dismantle it again he would not hear of it. He peered out at his barren World from inside it, sat down out of sight, weeping.

He was on his feet again, dabbing his eyes, when a bearded man in a black jacket climbed in the booth with him. He came in as if he owned the place. Marten's red face turned white.

"Gustave! You're back!"

"So is the World!"

They fell into each other's arms. Marten could feel the painter's bones poking through his jacket. He looked him in the eyes and saw there the months of dreamless nights, dreamless days. He could not bear to see his friend in such a state – thin and weak, so exhausted he looked ready to collapse. "All this time you found no work?" he said.

"No one wanted my visions, so I had none."

Marten swept a new canvas on the easel. "Here's one man who appreciates you! Here's one man who can't stand his World without you! From now on I want every piece of art you can churn out!"

Gustave crept toward the clean white canvas. "My work – my rest."

"Sweet dreams!" said Marten.

"Commission me!"

"I commission you!"

Marten stood around for a moment unsure of what to do with himself now that his big dream had come true. Then he rushed off.

Gustave stood motionless, gazing out over his canvas at the World come back to him. It was all set up but as yet unopened to the public, stock-still and silent, sitting for him. He thought his time apart from it had done him good. It was in rare focus. He breathed in deeply, picked up a good-sized brush. Frowning, he mixed some blue and red. A sad smile came to his face. "Sweet dreams." He began to smear.

His happy patron, returning with lemonade and two tickets for the roller coaster, found the painter swaying, swooning, deep into his dream.

David Daiches, 1938-1951

Remembering a Farm in East Lothian, Scotland

And if you find him standing on the soil
there, where the field slopes downward to the dyke,
you paint, of course, that summer years ago,
or that December night when, late from the hills,
you crushed the waiting snow
and hailed the shadow-throwing lights,
picked out the shining window, the warm kitchen smell.

Remembering the seasons and the pulse of life
you see him now: older, of course;
he has not joined the marchers, you'll not find him
looping the sky to peck the eyes from monsters
nor in the dark wash of the insidious seas
where limping ships grope sternly for the shore.
No, there he is, and if he shades his eyes
from the descending sun
he cannot turn again
and see the yellow window's compensation.

Night now is dead, or deadly,
never both: light from the open door
or undrawn blind is an earlier civilisation,
and, we have prayed, our children's heritage.

And yet the seasons live, and he with them.
Earth cannot dislocate the heavens
nor death so master life
that we must lose this vision with the rest.
Bound to the sun for warmth and light and love,
despising candles in the window,
now, a man with his former mistress,
ancient yet beautiful and charged with hope,
he remembers the old gods, smiling at the new
who will be neither old nor new, but living.
Seasons create, but what has time to do
with life? Love laughs at instruments.

Dirt on his boots is promise of our love;
corruption fosters life, but give it time.
Impermanent equilibrium of war
topples at last upon idolators
that feasted at those altars.

Reach out, reach out your hand to the revolving world
to touch the black that turns, despite us all,
to green. Memory, desire and love
shall yet negate these horrors.

We or our children, smiling at garden walls,
wistful under the moon, sunburned with love,
shall not remember that our friends have died,
nor any agony of the unknown loved,
but know they have escaped those barbed-wire views
to look through unborn eyes that gaze untaught
at the green turning world.

You or I or another …
some future perfect tense awaits us
and there we shall have smiled to see the sun
come down, yes, there, behind those very trees

(*Poetry* LIX, no VI, March 1942)

Scotland from America, 1938

Dull sky for wall in the east, but I look past,
knowing the neutral ocean lounges across,
and the travelling waves will totter home at last,
lapping into the little bays of Ross.

and if I greet you, you who are sad and apart,
whom history left after courting you a while,
will the Clyde be brighter for the warm wish of my heart,
will the Glasgow tenements fall, will Dundee smile?
And what of the folk at Kyle?

It is seven miles from Glenuig to the railway track,
and Macdonald the boatman has lost all the vigour he had,
and his two braw youngsters won't come sailing back:
no place in the glen for a lively lad.
(They were saying the wind was sad.)

If you have a handclasp for the miners of Fife,
what then? You have seen the sinister sun
slink behind slag-heaps and cottages. What of the life
of Tam at the corner? (Tam at the kirk!) Have done.
Not this time the English who won.

I know that the Castle Rock shines gay in the morning
(I remember): the undulant Princes Street crowds
do not seem to have read the strange notice of warning,
yes, written up high in the clouds
like banners – or shrouds.

I remember I drank cottage milk in Glen Falloch
(Just like that. There was nobody asked me to pay).
But there's refuse and oil in Loch Lomond at Balloch
and there's worse things than that by the Tay:
who will sweep it away?

Dull sky for eastern wall, but I look through
eastward and onward. Are the hills now clear?
If you climb (as I did) on the Pentlands, what of the view?
– Oh, in High Street pubs they chatter over beer:
come slow, new year. (*Poetry* LVII, no IV, January 1941)

On the Twelfth Day of Christmas I Screamed

(A letter from his girl to a GI in Tokyo)

Now April's here, whatever can I do
with those fantastic gifts I got from you?
Spring's in the air, but honey, life is hard:
the three French hens are pecking in the yard,
and the turtledove, the turtledove (one of them died) –
ah, love, my own true love, you have denied
me nothing the mails or the express could bring.
But look; we're into spring;
the calling birds are calling, calling;
the pear tree's leaves are slowly falling;
I sit here with those cackling geese
and never know a moment's peace.
My memories are mixed and hazy,
the drumming drummers drive me crazy,
the milking maids enjoy canasta,
the lords are leaping ever faster,
the pipers – God in Heaven knows
I've more than had enough of those.

My love, you do such wondrous things
(who else would think of *five* gold rings?)
I know you send me all you can
of spoils of occupied Japan,
but you remain on alien shore
and waiting here is such a bore.
My love, the lively lords are leaping:
some things will not improve with keeping.

Now April's here, the weary days go by;
I watch that wretched dove attempt to fly;
the partridge smells; the geese are getting hoarse;

my diction's growing positively coarse.
You must forgive my gestures of rejection –
I'm crazed with all your tokens of affection.
Enough's enough; next time be less romantic
and don't send gifts that drive a lady frantic.
Send me a postcard with a pretty view
And I shall look at it and think of you.
(*The New Yorker*, XXVII, no 9, 14 April 1951)

Season to Taste

When Jan is gone with winter snow
and Feb arrives (with winter snow)
we sadly watch the seasons go:
what are we thinking of?
Do we recall that gay recess,
that Christmas gave us all in Dec,
how shopping days grew daily less
since first announced in Nov?

How time has annually unlocked
its monthly stores which it keeps stocked
with (eg) autumn leaves in Oct
and back to school in Sept?
Have we, as winter moves to spring,
looked *on*, to what next month might bring,
or *back* with vain self-pitying
as hope or fear has leapt?

Do we reflect on reasons why
the heat in Aug is rarely dry
or how luxuriant July
triples the weeds of June?
Do we observe each shifting star,
or changing times of sunset – far
more wondrous than phenomena
like (say) the Harvest Moon?

The seasons have their annual sum
we know (well, roughly) what will come
from first primrose to latest plum
things move in ordered way.
If glance from Jan to Feb will not
reveal a change from cold to hot,
a walk to March might show a lot,
a March to April May.

DD through the ages (top-right, with his children; bottom-right, with Edwin Morgan)

Last Words

(on leaving the British Information Service, New York, 15 April 1944)

The time draws near when I shall make no more
the crowded swift ascent to this high floor,
no more to haunt these oft re-shuffled halls
where lust for information never palls.
There stern researchers strut with busy stride
passing the buck with skill from side to side,
where late the baffled expert sits alone
cursing each gruesome tinkle of the phone;
each finger of each trembling hand he crooks
marking a place in each of twenty books,
while telling *Newsweek, Time* and *Look* and *Life*
the age of some eccentric second wife,
the shade of Churchill's eyes, the King's pet cheese,
whether a peer removes his hat to sneeze.

Some things I shall rejoice to have remote:
no more re-writing what re-writers wrote
to have one's re-re-writing done again
by nameless forces in some hidden den.
No more compounding speeches by the bunch
for Fletcher to transmit to Elks at lunch …
Whitaker, Bible of th'Inquirer Section,
I shall no longer need your stern correction.
Farewell, O fact-filled volume. Farewell, too
O fair *Times* Index, you and I are through!

Henceforth if Facts elude me, I shall let 'em!
I'll call the BIS, by God, and get 'em!

From Chicago

I hae thocht o the shore o Fife an the sicht o the May
blinkin far ower the watter in morning shine;
och, lass, I hae thocht o the Anstruther boats the day,
an the strang smell o the sea, an mysel lang syne.

There was daffin doon by the rocks thae days, an fush
caught by a barefit callant under the stanes,
an the dulse thick i the haun, an the dowie hush
o the waves plashin at nicht, an the saft rains.

An the rasps on Kilrenny Common were smoor'd wi glory
when we went doon by the burn at sax i the morn,
wi the warl sleepin an the birdies chantin brawlie,
an the stowrie road losin itsel in the corn.

I shall spit frae the harbour waa at Pittenweem,
kick an auld tin doon the rumbling St Monans ways,
climb roon the Ness (this time it'll be nae dream)
frae Balconie sands tae Crail. Och, lassie, the days

are no sae lang as they were, we mauna bide,
for waur than bombs can deave a man thir days,
an it's no a man's brains or his siller that decide.
It's the sand an the stanes an the grass whaur the bairnie plays.

Spier eftir the dairgies that lie aff the rocks aa day,
spier eftir the reek that gaes up frae the lum at e'en,
spier eftir Fife, auld cronie o mines, an say
that ma bairns are coming tae play wi their faither's freen.

(*Poetry* LX, no V, August, 1942)

To My Brother, Lionel Henry Daiches

Here in the heat, an unco way frae hame,
I'm dowie wi remembering, like a fool,
lang syne when we were daft an young an skeigh,
crossing the Meedies on the way tae school.

Ye'll mind the grannies in the rocks at Crail,
the nichts we spun for mackerel oot-by Kyle,
or – later – at the Royal or Rutherford's,
in guid auld style.

Ay, we hae scrambled on the Pentland Hills,
we've reared Dunsappie tadpoles in a jar:
Cockenzie folk hae seen us lingering late
by the pools where the muckle partens are.

Och man, the nicht at Stirling we were fou!
Yon time we crossed Strome Ferry at peep o the sun!
An noo ye're a sodger and I – dinna laugh – a professor,
an oor wark's no done.

Ay man, it's a long fareweel tae the auld daft days,
the lichts hae gone oot on the shore an we canna see.
Scunnersome things are scrauchin in oor puir warld,
an they're lookin for you an me.

Here in the heat, an unco way frae hame,
I toast the yesterdays that time has torn,
an when Auld Reekie's lichts shine clear again
we'll drink thegither tae the morn's morn.

(Dedicatory poem from *Poetry and the Modern World*, 1940)

War Poem for Britain

When I say Plato, meaning bicycles,
dignified now through urgency and need,
I am not smiling, for this fruit has grown
from bitter seed.

I mention angels, catalogued as guns,
(no hope from doves or chubby, naked boys):
ours are the awkward engines that distil
silence from noise.

Ours is the laughter that, if heard not seen,
sounds like the brittle camouflage of tears;
our hopes can now be sighted through machines
and viewed as fears.

This is the land of Sundays, where the sound
of schoolgirl scales falls from accustomed rooms.
Yet this is music: flowers may flourish still
though grown on tombs.

Dear child, the spitfires move across the moon,
the symbols of our love are strange to read:
school is not easy where we learn to grow
laughter from dragon seed.

(*Poetry*, LXIII, No II, November 1943)

From *Chapman* 73

Flowers and Grocers

I took him for a drive in the car
when he was ninety-two, I less than half that.
He marvelled at the daffodils come round again,
and he still here. "Look," he said, "daffodils."
Is old age comforted by spring's return
or do we see renewal as for nature
and not for us? He was alive for one more spring
at least. The cruelty of that indifference
was felt by me and not by him.
I thought instead of how when we are gone
the round of life continues, grass and flowers and people,
buds appear, grow fat, burst out,
people follow their daily rounds, intent
on their own trivialities. Couples court by the river

as though they were immortal and unique.
He broke into these thoughts with exclamation.
"Look," he said, reading a village shop-sign slowly,
"J Thomson, family grocer."
He smiled, and said again "J Thomson, family grocer.
He is a family grocer," he told me,
Earnest and pleased. "J Thomson, family grocer.
That's nice," he added, settling in his seat,
touched by the ordinaryness.
I felt ashamed and moved. Why should this simple sign
of undistinguished human dailiness have touched him so?
Ninety-two he was, not long for this world,
this world of daffodils and family grocers.
Now myself well past the Psalmist's span
of seventy years I often think of this
and feel, surprisingly, a surge of love
for flowers and grocers everywhere.

Streaks

Observation with extensive view
said Dr Johnson, not numbering the streaks of the tulip.
Streaks of the tulip! What did he see
in his mind's eye when he used that phrase?
A tulip, streaked, stands sharply out
while all mankind from China to Peru
blur in a chain or do a strip-the-willow
or lose themselves in anthropology.
Short-sighted he was, streaked tulips
were too difficult. Mankind's the thing:
the mind copes, not the eye. Just representation
of general nature, he said.
Like parallel straight lines are straight lines
on the same plane that never meet
however far they are produced
in either direction.
But parallel lines do meet in the end
our universe being what we know it is,
and just representation is unjust
and mankind is man-unkind.
And Dr Johnson, wise, humane, sensible Dr Johnson,
was really, as Boswell showed, unique.
Observation with intensive view
showed all his streaks.
It is the streakiness that we remember.

Conductors

Tram conductors used to have machines
strapped to their chests and issued tickets
with a musical 'ping', a penny one,
a tuppenny or even a threepenny.
Progress has ended that.
On buses there are no conductors.
Give exact fare to the driver,
who presses buttons, pushes levers,
and then re-starts the bus.
The old conductors fumbled for change
in leather bags worn over the shoulder
and counted out the coins into your palm,
balancing like seamen as the tram lurched on.
Driving a tram was easy:
the rails carrying you where they led, but the conductor,
weighted and freighted with contraptions,
choosing a ticket – each with separate colour –
fitting the proper space to his machine,
punching the hole exactly,
climbing upstairs and downstairs on the swaying tram,
had a harder time.
Children went anywhere for a penny, a yellow ticket.
Red for a tuppenny, blue for a threepenny.
Those chromatic journeys live in my memory
like true adventures, true adventure stories,
the conductor always the hero.

Literary Criticism: Glasgow 1991

To be or not to fucking be,
that's the fucking question.
The silly cunt with the wee beard
spouting fucking literature.
Even Rabbie fucking Burns
wi his fucking suppers is no for me.
Fuck off, the lot o youse.

A Highbrow Version of the Above

The curfew tolls the knell of fucking day,
The fucking herd winds slowly o'er the lea,
The fucking ploughman homewards wends his way,
And leaves the darkening fucking world to me.

Reviews

Theatre Roundup, Autumn 2006

At the Edinburgh International Festival the National Theatre of Scotland (NTS) produced Realism, a play set in a morning of hangover in the life of one Paul Galloway, partly as happens in his head. Marshalling a strong Scottish cast Anthony Neilson worked in his favourite way, developing the script in rehearsal. This technique works well for him, producing work which inhabits both the characters' conscious and unconscious lives. In his other play, The Wonderful World of Dissocia, he gets us into the world of the profoundly disturbed in Realism. He confronts us with how 'un-normal', illogical and distorting so-called 'real life' is.

Paul is a typical human being fighting between higher purposes and hard-to-resist urges, his relationships are flawed, even with his near alter-ego Galloway, his cat, whose physical body language comments on his master's almost random life. Across the stage his girl fiend, her sister, his parents and friends appear as he'd like to encounter them. Set in today's tough environment and Paul's rich fantasy life, the male audience responded with understanding and recognition, while many women sighed with the exasperation borne of experience with their own Pauls, being close to men who want to live their fantasies for real. This isn't sexist: in fact the responses show how in touch people are with their own inner geography.

The fascinating Dissocia will be touring in the Spring. These two plays, if staged as a double bill, would interact interestingly as they dramatically explore the way we wander, detected or undetected, far away from the boundaries of normality. The set, lighting and music composition for both were designed by Miriam Buether, Chahine Yavroyan and Nick Powell respectively, their approach in Reality beautifully book- ending their creation in the other production, an atmosphere of somewhere other.

At the still-intimate but redesigned Netherbow aka The Scottish Storytelling Centre, Rowan Tree Theatre Company Fringe production was John Carnegie's new play Hermiston, based on the unfinished novel by RLS. He shifts the time from 1813 to 1792 and uses many of the attitudes and sayings expressed in broad, rough Scots by Lord Justice Clerk Braxfield, the infamous judge on whom Stevenson's fictitious character was based. This enables Carnegie to make the play resonate with present day Scotland where there are signs of a resurgence in the language, (in 1792 it was being eroded from formal society in favour of English) and of the re-emergence of the Scots, as, hopefully, an increasingly self governing people.

The richly Scots-tongued actor Michael Mackenzie played Hermiston, silver-voiced in text or song, Isabella Jarrett the servant and Grant O'Rourke the judge's son. They ensured that we saw the passion for what individuals see as their culture, be we Scots tongued or no. Many new plays are based in our recent past, often trapping the play's potential power. The novel's 19th century setting is sharply focussed on cultural decay and endangerment on the one hand, but there are also hints of the underlying robustness and resilience of cultural identity then – and many parallels which help us to understand our dangers and opportunities now.

NTS brought two plays to Edinburgh in August. Set in the Drill Hall in Forrest Road, Gregory Burke's Black Watch was powerfully directed by John Tiffany. Revivals of excellent productions are becoming a welcome feature here. This sold-out show will be revived in the Spring so there is another opportunity to see what others of many ages and experience raved about.

September, and A Play A Pie and A Pint managed to try out an Edinburgh Season taking the Glasgow plays east for a second week at the Jam House. Resident Edinburgh audiences are more cautious than Glasgow ones.

By the end of the season it revealed an audience for lunchtime theatre but we could do with a space where they could linger before and afterwards as in the venture's Glasgow's home, Oran Mor in Byres Road.

Tir Nan Og by Dave Anderson was the most notable of the plays brought by PPP. Myra McFadyen took the lead role of 'The Woman', her voice and movement superbly in tune with the emot-ional depth of both script and music. The Woman sang bitter, funny lyrics as she moved from her small flat to work as a singer on a North Sea ferry in winter – "In a civilised society everyone's an artist, everyone's a star". Then she moved to "hawking her cabookee in the port of Amsterdam". The mature woman's journey takes her into the sea to be with the undead you never grow old with and to the Land of the Young with its raft of possibilities.

With Allan Tall leading the musicians, including fiddler Jennifer Rhodes who also acted the other characters, the short musical delight contained songs that lodged themselves in the memory. Directed by Adrian Osmond, McFadyen's central performance as the older woman still full of possibilities brought tears to the eyes. It was a vision of how satisfying the short intense dramatic form can be, Anderson should develop the Tir Nan Og's style further, a new-century development from his 7:84 work, making political comment with even wryer humour.

The NTS also had a musical drama with John Byrne's stage version of the much-loved 1980's TV series Tutti Frutti directed by Tony Cownie. Starring Dawn Steele as Suzy Kettles with a strong cast including John Ramage as Eddie Clockerty, Tom Urie as Danny McGlonie, Tam Dean Burn as Vincent and Julie Wilson Nimmo as Miss Toner, the three venues used its first tour were full booked. Sometimes people can be scathing about popular entertainment, but NTS achieved a production of sharp quality. Just as well, the love Scots bear those characters was tangible in the audience reaction. Like several other of the NTS productions this will tour in the Spring and is already virtually sold out in Glasgow at least.

The Traverse took advantage of having three stages for the 2006 Fringe and continued to use the spaces in the autumn. They managed to produced a mini-season, Cubed3, with three short commissioned plays under the banner Tilt, using the same cast and director. They also gave two companies space to devise two plays and several other associated events.

In Tilt David Priestley's White Point wasn't sufficiently sharp to hold attention, confusing rather than intriguing the audience. Yet another play about the lostness of those in their thirties, a theme which needs more than realistic dialogue to justify its time on stage. By contrast Broke, Iain F MacLeod's version of David Lascot original French play Un Homme en Failite, was a sophisticated, surreal experience of a Man, David Ireland, whose life spirals out of his control after his partner, Woman Abigail Davis, leaves and the Designated Liquidator, Garry Collins comes to sort the mess out.

Morna Pearson's Distracted had Annie Lacey joining the trio of actors as Granny, a woman whose grasp on reality had long slackened. The setting is a caravan park in the North East where Granny arrives with Jamie her grandson, played with wonderfully troubling edge by Collins. Already there is George Michael, played by also by David Ireland, a boy trying to understand his world and his parent's. Bunny, his mother, is more a child than a mother herself. Using North Eastern rhythms and accents new playwright Pearson created a many textured play filled with black humour and disturbing incidents as the boys reveal how hard they try to make a sensible world out of the disintegrating fragments their "in need of help themselves" carers increasingly struggle to provide. Lorne Campbell's direction drew notable performances from the very talented cast.

As a way of enabling us to see more of the new playwrights the Traverse develops, including visual art and music, the Cubed3

Season is an interesting development. Unfortunately neither of the two devising companies, Highway Diner or 12 Stars and the Pastels produced very striking work, and their 15 Minutes and Do I Mean Anything, clearly did not have enough time to evolve.

Playwrights and Companies in Scotland need to engage not only those who come of their own freewill, but also children. For the over-eights, Nicola McCartney provided the text for Catherine Wheels' The Lion of Kabul. The audience were led in and seated around the sides of a yurt-style structure to meet a lion, Marjan, who lived most of his life in Kabul Zoo. Marjan was played by artistic director Gill Robertson, and his keeper Akbhar by Kieran Cheung who also provided the music. Other animals and characters were created by images projected on the upper walls of the tent as we experienced the growing Marjan, the life of the Zoo, the hostilities outside in the mountains and then in the city as bombs fell and life changed.

The young audience were gently drawn in to a play which didn't flinch to show the damage wars do or how age reduces what any creature can do. Performed with the audience around, the emotions more easily experienced – a reminder that Scotland needs to develop more flexible spaces.

David Greig wrote Yellow Moon, published by Faber, For TAG, aimed at the teenage audience and containing the most beautifully crafted dialogue. Greig's highly tuned, sensitive but modern text reads well on the page making this reviewer wish events had enabled her to see the production as well. Published texts should be more readily available, the Playwrights Studio in Glasgow runs an online shop at playwrightsstudio.co.uk but they can only sell what is published. The Tilted plays, unlike the Traverse plays that preceded them, were unfortunately not printed. Theatres could to explore online print.

The Tron, despite not having Forbes Masson's writer input, presented another modern Panto set in Pantoland, Wullie Whittington, co-written by Gordon Dougall and Fletcher Mather. In the tradition of Tron Pantos there were jokes at the expense of the other theatres including NTS, but the new writing team ducked taking as sharp digs at the general Scottish scene as Forbes used to.

Several Scottish panto-smiths got their digs at our local scene: with Jim Chisholm ugly sistering and scripting Perth Theatre's Cinderella with Ian Grieve. Liam Rudden successfully delivered his first Panto for the Brunton while Alan McHugh supplied several to venues – and appeared at Aberdeen. In Glasgow and Edinburgh the fully Scottish freshly-written show at their King's Theatres has yet to occur this century, though Allan Stewart brought new text and 'female charms' to Edinburgh King's 100th Anniversary show with flying doves, live ponies and snow falling on the audience at the end.

At the Royal Lyceum Director Mark Thomson staged his new version of Carlo Collodi's tale of the wooden puppet who becomes a boy after many sometimes-dire adventures. Sticking largely to the original's more robust story, there was no Disney-feel-good factor here, more the painful side of life seen through larger than life Commedia dell Arte acting. James Anthony Pearson gave the role of Pinocchio a real sense of the danger and vulnerability of the wee puppet while Andy Clark, Molly Innes and Matthew Pigeon fully created their several characters including, for Clark, a sly fox, Innes an eerie Toyland driver and Matthew a very camp poodle and a pragmatic Green Fisherman. To the disappointment of some the production was high on morals rather than festive fun.

Audiences require a mix of things from productions, characters to love and understand as well as good staging, tight scripts and productions. Some fun too helps draw audiences back – sophisticated as in Broke, sharp-edged as in Distracted or poking fun at our present day as in several of the others mentioned here. Scots can still be overly earnest, dour in fact and in our arts we need to cast off more of our Calvinist brakes to set our imaginations free. *Thelma Good*

Pamphleteer

An old hand at producing pamphlets, the ever-reliable Smith/Doorstop (The Poetry Business, The Studio, Byram Arcade, Westgate, Huddersfield) has produced Jane Routh's *Teach Yourself Map Making*, Ed Reiss's *Now Then* and Hugh McMillan's *After the Storm*. Containing a broad range of style and poetic voice, *Teach Yourself ...* (£7.95) has an evocative delicacy and depth which Routh has pouring from nautical description and jargon. From the opening poem, 'a beautiful art':

> The pencil soft, but finely pointed.
> A quiet clack of parallel rules;
> the marks on paper light, transient.
> Erased by evening.

With a chance encounter with a cow at sea and rolling waves galore, this is suitable reading for rounding the Corryvreckan!

In Ed Reiss's *Now Then* (£3.00), the well constructed verses stand for themselves. The thought-provoking 'Wrong Man' imbues a deft comic touch into a simple rustic style that is light and finely- balanced. Combining sly humour with a robust approach to one concepts of 'Englishness', Reiss is by turns subtle and engaging. 'Homage to Hieronymus Bosch' is a rich, sensory piece evoking a rich, sensory "Garden of Earthly Delights" which "hung beside your bed, where we embracing slept,/ emparadised, among luscious berry-globules,/ humungous fruits, popinjay, riot and lake.

Marking a student's work while in the pub is not necessarily advisable, however tempting for a teacher faced with a mound of papers. Hugh McMillan does it nevertheless in *After the Storm* (£3.00) and drily notes in 'Marked' that "ten pints can leave in tatters/ the critical apparatus". Not half it can't. McMillan elsewhere glumly muses that there are "no more multiples of forty-eight" in his likely lifespan, but the overall gloom is shot through with a nicely lyrical touch that leavens it, bringing it toward contemplation rather pure miseryguts stuff.

William Gault Bonar's *Frostburn Steel* is for the industrial heart, for snow-covered farmland, and for summer evenings in the inner city (see 'Bluid Brithers' and 'Snow Storm'). The title refers to blow-torched metal in the shipyards, and the industrial heartland is the primary focus of WGB's attention. He presents us with his usual high standard of writing in thoughtful, whimsical vein. Dreadful Night (82 Kelvin Court, Gt Western Road, Glasgow) have produced a delightful opus here for only £5.00.

Not satisfied with that, Dreadful Night have also produced Alan Gay's *The Boy Who Came Ashore* (£5.00). A powerful and insightful exploration of the devastating effects of an east coast storm in 1881, Gay's poetic vision is enhanced with primary sources, including weather reports, and is all the more powerful for it. The storm described ravaged the east coast of Britain, and Eyemouth and Burnmouth alone lost a third of the adult male population as they went down in their fishing boats. These poems are tonal and onomatopoeic – and evocative too of the daily sound of the fishing communities as in 'Hauling'

> Each net hauls a cran
> salt burned fingers lock in mesh
> decks thump with silver

A sensory evocation of life, with statements and voices from differing perspectives – it is obvious Gay has a gift for history as well as for poetry. *The Boy Who Came Ashore* is wonderful collaboration complemented by sensitive work – not to be missed.

Vane Women (Darlington Arts Centre, Vane Terrace, Darlington) has taken full advantage of the range possible in the two pamphlets *burning the blue winged boys* (sic) by Chris Powell, and *the right amount of vinegar* by Margaret Rule. Powell's work is a compilation of short stories: though not a breathtaking new dimension to the world of short story writing, here is a highly readable pamphlet, well worth £4.00 of your cash!

A photograph of a 1940s kipper salesman adorns the cover of *the right amount of vinegar* (£4.00), and suitably sets the scene for Yorkshire meditations. A eulogy for reading poetry, 'Books at Evening', makes a positive, upbeat start to the collection encouraging you to enjoy bite-size chunks of poetry on captivating themes. The eponymous poem is a short but timeless description of an scrumptious Sunday lunch; an epicurean addition to a pastoral collection. The description is so mouth-watering you almost need a knife and fork!

Oystercatcher (4 Coastgaurd Cottages, Lighthouse Close, Old Hunstanton, Norfolk) presents *Minor Yours* and *Sound Signals Advising of Presence*, both by Peter Hughes (£3.00 each). Although both classily presented, *Minor Yours* catches the eye for its sharpness and concision. Although the description is of almost uniform drabness – "we skewer artichoke hearts/ in the tin & watch the electric fire" there is a keen awareness of a life beyond Aldi, Sense shops and miserable evenings spent indoors. A reflective collection well worth a peek.

The poems in *Sound Signals* depart from Hughes's approach in *Minor Yours*, here favouring linear progression to a succession of images. Despite this, too many of these poems are over-short. More development is deserved, and the product is forced. Hughes is still able to capture a state of mind, though:

> First July light covered our sea with birds.
> More than ever before rode the morning,
> moving with a rhythm from the distance –
> the bay, the chalk & sandstone,
> the moon's ghost.

With SCPSW's anthology of civil servants writing in *Waves 2006* (£2.50 from 19 Arkley Court, Maidenhead) there is a determination, as in Sylvia Newmann's 'Mushrooms', to produce resonant images:

> Mushrooms of spectral hues or phallic forms
> Emerge like mythic monsters from decay.

With any anthology, there is inevitably a mixed-bag feel to the affair, but editor Liz Rowlands keeps a steady hand on the tiller, ensuring that this motley crew (if you're allowed to call civil servants that!) into an orderly and fulfilling read.

Akros (33 Lady Nairn Avenue, Kirkcaldy) meanwhile have harnessed the formidable talents of William Hershaw to produce *Fifty Fife Sonnets: Coarse and Fine* (£3.25). Whether in Scots or English, Hershaw captures a raw sense of worth and continually stirs up new dimensions, as in 'The Werewolf of Langtoun'

> Last nicht I broke in Nairn's that's been lang shut
> tae chore a length o leid an ither things,
> the rest o them were feard and widnae but
> they swore they'd speirt a ghaist in there, …

Akros also champions George Philp and his *Confessions of an Occasional Poet* (£3.25). Philp writes in a raw, but thought-provoking style, further abetted by his notes on the poetry. Most of the poetry is in combative Scots (as are the tributes by other poets), with a real meaty taste to it, as in William Neill's 'Doctor George Philp':

> I heard a chiel yince cry ye Doc Rigbane
> He tellt me hou ye'd caa't his spondyls back
> intil thair am richt bit. White care ye'd tak
> tae pit his sair nesh banes tae wark again.

Faber (3 Queen Square, London) have gone for a more sober approach with Harold Pinter's *War* (£5.00). No subtlety, no compromise, no bullshit: Pinter is as uncompromising as ever on the topic of conflict, pouring scorn on his favourite targets, the Americans. While it's invigorating to read something as direct as this, the lack of subtlety brings with it the air of Pinter exercising personal prejudices – westerners waging war: bad, bad men whatever you do; Palestinians, al-Quaeda *et al*: since you're fighting against western imperialism, it's all right to kill anyone you choose. Still, it really gets the mind working, if only to counter some of his more outlandish statements – while Bush and Blair deserves much condemnation, it's going just a little too far to say that the responsibility for a terrorist attack on the London Undergound "will rest entirely on the shoulders of our Prime Minister". Isn't that letting the Muslim equivalents of the KKK and, alas, all too many others, completely off the hook?

Larry Butler's *Han Shan Everywhere* (£5.00, Survivor's Press, 2/R 5 West Bank Quadrant, Glasgow) is a pastoral exercise in eastern spiritualism and the west of Scotland. Declaring his inspiration to be the Chinese writer Han Shan, Butler writes about nothing very much – walks in the country, killing time – and imbues it with a meaning beyond "wearing marigolds to pr-vent stings". Even waiting in the post office queue brings a chance for contemplation! So, if you see a man looking dreamy in the queue ahead of you, don't worry: it's just Butler getting in touch with his inner being.

Martin Bates paints a vivid, tangible depiction of Nicaragua in *Exploding Cicadas* (£3.50, White Adder Press, Lynn Cottage, East Linton, East Lothian). Created while on sabbatical in the rural north of the country, it's a delicate evocation of a life far removed from our own, whether it's watching a soapy *telenovela* on a TV powered by car battery, or standing on a verandah, waiting for rain. While it's sometimes hard to get past the excellently-turned description into something deeper, the pen portraits are a joy to behold. 'On the Verandah' gives a nice flavour of the collection:

Rain in the offing – the little boy runs
swinging Professor Michael's fly-swat.
My notebooks strewn around loom as I stare.
Along the concrete edge a line of plants
stand to attention their green arms sloped
red plumes waving from their tips.

By the way, the cicadas of the title are wee insects who come out once every 17 years to mate: we have it on good authority the din they make is earsplitting!

Published by Mariscat (10 Bell Place, Edinburgh), Into Glasgow, is an anthology of "translations and responses" to works of art from *Hamlet* to *Cyrano de Bergerac*, all expressed in feisty Glaswegian dialect. The offerings here from pens as various as Tom Leonard, Edwin Morgan and Stephen Mulrine may take a little practice to read but they are certainly forthright and hard-hitting. (William Carlos Williams will never seem the same after Leonard's treatment of him.) A terrific read as well as a powerful apologia for an undersung dialect, crowned with Adam McNaughtan's 'Oor Hamlet' which has become one of our best-loved songs.

A Sound Companion to the Scottish Poems of Robert Fergusson is a little unwieldy as a title for a small pamphlet like George Philp's (yes, you can't put a good man down!), but the The Scots Language Society (Blackford Lodge, Blackford, Perthshire) deserves kudos for a highly academic treatment of a poet often seen as inspiration for Burns. Philp amply shows that Fergusson deserves consideration on his own merits. A running translation of the more difficult phrases in his work is displayed, thus removing hurdles for the novice. The words spring to life, after more than two centuries, with 'The King's Birthday in Edinburgh' being typical:

I sing the day sae aften sung,
Wi which our lugs hae yearly rung,
In whase loud praise the Muse has dung
An kind o print;
But wow! The limmer's fairly flung;
There's naething in't.

The Crowlin Press (482 Clarkston Road, Netherlee, Glasgow) meanwhile publishes Alan MacGillivray's pamphlet; *Kindly Clouds*. Thematically, these poems are reflective and abstract, but there is a firm grip on the material that lends a truly earthy feel to them: In 'Black and White':

This is how that past remains awake.
After the memories shrug on their macs
And go out into the dark rain,
And all the voices stumble up the stairs
Towards their pillow whispering,

Donny O'Rourke calls him 'a clown who can play Hamlet' and on this reading, we can well believe him, despite MacGillivray name-dropping O'Rourke in one of the pieces!

A quick mention of Tom Murray's *The Future is Behind You* (£2.50, Lapwing Press, Lower Kirklands, The Glebe, Selkirk) – the encounter with Neal Cassady's widow, forever carrying his memory, alone, merits the modest price! *Jonathan Washington*

Catalogue 109

"It was unsafe to walk the streets of Edinburgh at night, on account of the numerous drunken parties of young men who reeled about, bent on mischief at all hours". Not a description of today's city, but of Edinburgh over 200 years ago – *plus ça change*! This and other nuggets are on show in Ralph Lownie's *Auld Reekie: An Edinburgh Anthology* (Timewell, £12.99). Taking on diverse subjects – Edinburgh people, pastimes, wartime and ... Lownie gamely disproves MacDiarmid and Grassic Gibbon's gloomy verdict that any anthology about Edinburgh would be "an exceedingly slim volume indeed". Although the city does come over as a little high-falutin', the book's still well worth a delve through.

While the past is on display in Lownie's version, it's the future that concerns *Scotland 2020* (Luath, £9.99). A wide range of figures peer into their crystal balls, from disgraced former First Minister Henry McLeish to Elaine C Smith (who loves her exclamation marks!!). Two highlights: Iain Docherty's plea for an integrated transport policy, and Sally Daghtian pointing out Scotland has always welcomed refugees, from St Columba onwards. But in a broad exercise like this, whole communities and issues disappear through the cracks, even under editor Kenny MacAskill's eagle eye. What about Scotland's gay population? Whither Scots language? But a thought-provoking read, especially when the Labour Party is ettling to scare voters into not voting SNP in May.

Another anthology of Scottish poetry? Egads! But here is *The Edinburgh Book of Twentieth-Century Scottish Poetry* (EUP, £19.99), large as life and twice as real. Editors Maurice Lindsay and Lesley Duncan provide a neat counter-point: Lindsay the patrician pillar of the establishment (*sixty* years since he edited *Modern Scottish Poetry*), Duncan the voice of a younger generation. There's all the (un)usual suspects – MacDiarmid, MacCaig, MacLean and so on – but also a strong female presence, many never widely praised before, like Siùsaidh NicNèill. It's also notable for its even-handed treatment of poetry in English, Scots and Gaelic. At less than twenty quid for a handsome, lengthy edition, it's excellent value for a primer on Scottish poetry.

Like Scottish poetry, the Scots language has been studied in an attempt to solidify it against the creeping barrage of the Angles. *The Essential Scots Dictionary* (EUP/ Scottish Language Dictionaries, £7.99) is the latest episode in a handy size, designed for those who don't already have a Scots dictionary (or two) to hand. It's a reminder of how lively and combative the language is, from 'scaffie' (a street-sweeper) to 'footer' (to dawdle or engage in trivial activity) and something to consult whenever you plunge into an obscure lexical backwater. The more academic *Perspectives on the Older Scottish Tongue* (EUP, £25.00) shows how essential Scots was in the past in all walks of life – from the legal system to village gossip.

Although there's been an upswing in Scots novels, there's nothing like hearing it in person. *Serving Twa Maisters* (EUP, £12.50) celebrates the continuing use of Scots in the theatre, with five plays translated from Brecht to Molière. Hector MacMillan observes: "we do seem to share a very European enjoyment of abrupt transitions of mood in our writings". Scots is ideally suited to translations because of its earthy connectiveness to reality. Long may it continue. Two other theatrical books act as contrast: *Rough Guide to Shakespeare* by Andrew Dickson (Rough Guides, £14.99) is a lively romp through Shakey's work for the beginner, including sharp analysis and pointed reviews. C P Taylor's *North* (Methuen/Iron, £5.95) is a collection of six works by the extremely versatile playwright. Hardly remembered outside professional circles, it's high time for a revival of his keenly-observed social dramas.

Now in his seventies, Hector MacMillan hasn't slowed down. With a successful life in the theatre under his belt, he has written a biography of the radical Thomas Muir in *Handful of Rogues* (Argyll, £15.99). Although nowhere near as well known as Messrs Wallace and Bruce, MacMillan makes a compelling case for adding Muir to this pantheon. After all, Muir made a reasoned, carefully-put case for constitutional reform after seeing corruption all around him in 1790s Scotland. Only problem was that after 1745 and more recently the French Revolution, the authorities were decidedly jittery about any threat to their power, no matter how reasonable it was. After a joke of a trial, Muir was found guilty of sedition and transported to Australia for 14 years. In an era where authorities crack down on anyone posing a threat to the status quo, this makes for a fascinating but troubling read.

"I was convinced our Heavenly Father was none other than the Director General of the Italian State Railway company" – one of many delightful thoughts passing through the young Dario Fo's mind, as chronicled in *My First Seven Years (and a Few More)* (Methuen, £14.99). This is a soft-focus, soft-centre book with the emphasis firmly on nostalgia, although growing up next to Lake Maggiore in the Italian Alps would be pretty idyllic for anyone. The Nobel Prize-winning author makes it all magical, childish hi-jinks and all. Hard to believe that in the same country Il Duce was strutting his stuff.

Another memoir, though decidedly less chronological, is Jenni Daiches' *Not Nebuchadnezzar* (Luath, £9.99). Taking on the form of separate but related essays on subjects such as names (Daiches is aka Jenni Calder), Judaism, Scottish identity and many others. The reputation of her father, the redoubtable polymath David Daiches, inevitably cast a shadow over her, although not as much as you would think. Her differing experiences – born in Chicago, growing up in the US and Scotland, and working for the Museum of Scotland has meant that personal and national identity become one and the same to a intriguing degree. Although the blurb characterises this as a "life study" rather than autobiography, this is a learned, thoughtful book, to help anyone unsure of who they are. So a wide audience then!

Identity is also a key concern for Tom Nairn and Paul James in *Global Matrix: Nationalism, Globalism and State-Terrorism* (Pluto, £16.99). Musing on the seemingly inevitable expansion of globalisation and nationalism, Nairn and James don't automatically dismiss nationalism as the bogeyman of Bush, Milosevic and Hussein *et al* but call for a "civic nationalism" where a nation chooses to fight against its prejudices and base instincts, instead of embracing them. While the enemies of 'civic nationalism' may be many and varied (from the BNP to the more disreput-able end of the media) – they can be defeated by a larger, enlightened alliance of people and government. It's not all doom and gloom, but it does require you to get up off yer bum and *do* something. Great stuff, even if the part about nationalism/national*ism*/*national*ism goes a little over our heads.

One key expression of national identity enjoying a resurgence today is the telling of folk tales: William and Norah Montgomerie's *The Well at the End of the World* (Mercat, £12.99) is a treasure trove of Scotland's stories. Inhabiting a fantastical realm of kings and queens, ogres, and mermaids, the deceptively-simple language reveals much about morality, the nature of good and evil, and more – from tales like 'Green Kirtle' and 'The Winning of Hyn-Hallow'. You'll be tempted to read it yourself after giving the kids their bedtime story. If nothing else, you'll learn the value of being nice to ponies and scaly men!

A possible companion volume, but much more learned is *The Book of the Cailleach* (Cork University Press, €49.00), an analysis of the 'wise woman' figure in Irish folklore, alongside the stories them-selves. Gearóid Ó Crualaoidh delves deep into the background and culture these stories sprang from, and argues that, not just giving entertainment round a fire on a cold night, these stories acted as therapy for the listeners. An absorbing delve into the world of *Cailleach*, a keenly-drawn female figure – quite a difference from the rather macho worlds of Beowulf and Odin. If you want to know why babies can't walk until they're two, read on.

The Scots' relationship to drink has often been one of quantity rather than quality, as any trip round night-time Scotland will attest. Phillip Hills, one of at least some with a more discerning palates is one such champion of great *uisge beatha*, and in *The Scottish Whisky Directory* (Mainstream, £15.99) he ably separates the golden nectar from the paint-stripper, and applies a rigorously undogmatic approach to the stuff – blended malts, for instance, don't receive the automatic thumbs down that a single malt purist would give them. Whisky snobs might want to sit down before they hear this, but The Famous Grouse blend gets a rave review here – setting the cat amongst the pigeons!

A different kind of drink is evidenced by *The Scots at Sea* (Saint Andrew Press, £19.99) – and it shares the straight approach of the whisky book, telling the story of the Scots who took to the water, from shipbuilders of Aberdeen and Glasgow, to sailors in the Royal Navy. Simply told, but gripping reading – especially about clippers racing each other from Shanghai on the tea run, you can almost taste the sea spray. But it's the lesser-known tales that illuminate most – like how Clyde-built steamships dashed contraband past the Union blockade in the US Civil War. A great read, even if you've only sailed a rubber ducky in the bath.

Last mentions: *Cookin'* (SNIP, £10.00), a collection of yummy recipes by celeb musos from Eddi Reader to Roddy Woomble. All in the aid of SNIP, which supports parents and carers of children with special needs, with an intro by *Chapman* 108 cover star Ian Rankin. Also unmissable is Paul Anderson's 1,360-page(!) *Hunger's Brides* (Carroll & Graf, $35.00). It's a terrific read, and we don't just say that because it started life as a short story in *Chapman* 80!

Edmund O'Connor

Notes on Contributors

Meg Bateman: Born Edinburgh, 1959. Learned Gaelic in S Uist and Aberdeen University where she also taught for many years. Has published two poetry collections and several anthologies.

David Betteridge: a teacher (retired) and has written poems for 40 years. Inspirations include Glasgow, and writers Blake and MacDiarmid..

Frances Campbell: means 'freedom' and 'wry-mouth' – qualities she delights in using simultaneously. Once worked in a call centre as 'Caroline', which helped win over angry people.

Stewart Conn: latest poetry collections include *Stolen Light* and *Ghosts at Cockcrow*. He has also published plays, a memoir, *Distances*, and *100 Favourite Scottish Poems* (ed) (Luath/SPL).

David Daiches (1912-2005): scholar and critic; led revival of Scottish literary studies. Published poetry in *Poetry* and *The New Yorker*, collection: *A Weekly Scotsman* (Black Ace, 1994).

Christine De Luca: writes in English and Shetlandic. Four poetry collection, recently *Parallel Worlds* (Luath). Bilingual collection (French) due 2007. Convener, Shore Poets.

Gavin Dunlop: survivor of a Civil Service career; writes poetry to voice what he feels without interruption from what he doesn`t. Other vices: crime (novels), coke (diet) and California.

Robert Ewing: Edinburgh GP, writing for 10 years – short stories and a novel. Keeps busy, doesn't drink too much and is afflicted by 'pattern balding'. Favourite star sign: Copernicus.

W D Fyfe: has worked as radio scriptwriter and producer in USA and Canada, also magazine staff writer and editor. Living in Vancouver, writing freelance and working on a novel.

Charlie Gracie: from Baillieston, land of poets – lives Thornhill. Work in *Cutting Teeth*, *New Writing Scotland* and *The Herald*. Is after what glimmers on (or lurks just beneath) the surface.

Richard King: PhD candidate in School of English, St Andrews. Author of several articles on maritime topics. Working on debut novel.

Norman Kreitman: lives in Edinburgh, has published a book on metaphor and related essays. Three poetry books – *Touching Rock, Against Leviathan* and *Casanova's 72nd Birthday*.

Brian Lamont: born and studied in Edinburgh, MA Hons Eng literature. Recently obtained an MA in Culture and Communication from UEA.

Donald Mackay: Pamphlet, *Kept in the Dark* (Mariscat), out this autumn. A book, *Elementary* (Dreadful Night), due soon. Lives in Caithness, and regularly falls off the edge of Scotland.

Kevin McEneaney: author of *Runic Tongue, The Enclosed Garden* and *Longing*. Co-editor of the *Irish Literary Supplement* and consultant in world literature to *Encyclopedia Americana*.

Colin Nicholson: Professor of 18th century and Modern Literature at Edinburgh University. Currently updating *Poem, Purpose and Place: Shaping Identity in Contemporary Scottish Verse* (1992) for electronic publication.

Zerrin Otgur: Born on road, 1971. Turned philosopher from lack of formal schooling. Infected by writing disease, 1998. Convalescing with pen and paper in Europe ever since. Many lines to go.

Richard Price: Recent books *Lucky Day* (Carcanet) and versions of French poet Louise Labé, *Lute Variations* (Rack Press). Head of Modern British Collections at the British Library.

David Purves: born Selkirk. Special interest in Scots orthography. Many poems in magazines. Three plays, inc *The Puddok an the Princess*, (Fringe First winner) produced by Theatre Alba.

Tessa Ransford: established poet, translator, editor and cultural activist campaigning for last 30 years. Founder Scottish Poetry Library – recent President, Scottish PEN.

Elizabeth Reeder: born Chicago, Glasgow since 1994 (likes second cities). Widely published and broadcast; teaches creative writing.

Julie-ann Rowell: Pamphlet Convergence was Poetry Book Society Choice. First prize in The New Writer Poetry Competition for a short collection; has MA in Creative Writing.

John Sampson: Edinburgh musician, composer and actor. Theatrical triumphs include *Black Sun Over Genoa*. Plays many flutes – fantastic legs – see them on www.johnsampson.co.uk!

Julie Stradner: teacher/trainer, worked in Sweden, Turkey and the Republic of Georgia. Won *Woman and Home* short story prize in 2001; work in *Dark Tales* and *The London Magazine*.

Todd Swift edited the CD *Life Lines: Poets for Oxfam*. Poems in *The Guardian*, *Poetry Review*, *The London Magazine* and *Poetry London*. Core Tutor for The Poetry School.